RESIDENTIAL HOUSING AND NUCLEAR ATTACK

BUILDING AND SOCIAL HOUSING FOUNDATION

Building and Social Housing Foundation is a research and education institute based in Coalville, Leicestershire.

It has been endowed with funds by a building organisation formed by a group of homeless and penniless ex-servicemen just after World War II, who were determined not just to solve their own housing problem, but to assist others in similar circumstances.

A study prepared by the United Nations Industrial Development Organisation suggested their methods and organisation could be adapted or replicated in the developing countries.

Building and Social Housing Foundation has established connections worldwide and research projects have been carried out in India, Tanzania, Ethiopia, Kenya and Poland as well as in the United Kingdom. Emphasis in all projects has been on self-help and self-reliance and on a reduction in state bureaucracy and control.

The Foundation is especially concerned to look to the future in a progressive and imaginative way, and to attempt to identify ways in which residential housing will need to be adapted in a rapidly changing world. Of particular interest is the need to identify a sustainable and viable way of life for the future in both the developed and developing world.

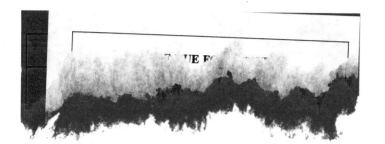

Residential Housing and Nuclear Attack

Diane Diacon

CROOM HELM
London • Sydney • Dover, New Hampshire

© 1984 Diane Diacon
Croom Helm Ltd, Provident House, Burrell Row,
Beckenham, Kent BR3 1AT
Croom Helm Australia Pty Ltd, First Floor, 139 King Street,
Sydney, NSW 2001, Australia

British Library Cataloguing in Publication Data

Diacon, Diane
    Residential housing and nuclear attack.
    1. Housing – Great Britain – Effect of
    atomic warfare on
    I. Title
    363.5'0941   HD7333.A3
    ISBN 0-7099-0868-7

cc 314097

Croom Helm, 51 Washington Street,
Dover, New Hampshire, 03820 USA

Library of Congress Cataloging in Publication Data

Diacon, Diane, 1954-
    Residential housing and nuclear attack.

    Bibliography: p. 139
    Includes index.
    1. Nuclear warfare. 2. Great Britain – Civil defense.
3. Housing – Great Britain. I. Building and Social
Housing Foundation (Coalville, Leicestershire).
II. Title.
U263.D5   1984   363.3'5   84-17639
ISBN 0-7099-0868-7

Printed and bound in Great Britain by
Biddles Ltd, Guildford and King's Lynn

CONTENTS

FIGURES

TABLES

ACKNOWLEDGEMENTS

I would like to acknowledge the help of all those who assisted in the preparation of this book — in particular I should like to thank all those local authorities, building societies and commercial firms who responded to requests for information, the Home Office for provision of detailed information as well as current policy guidelines, Dr Peter Branson for his guidance on matters of nuclear physics and various academic sources for advice on other technical matters.

Diane Diacon

1 INTRODUCTION

The Civil Defence Review set out in Home Office circular No. ES1/1981 states clearly that 'Because of the prohibitive cost of providing purpose-built public shelters it remains the Government's policy to explain to people how to provide practical protection in their own homes.'

The purpose of this book is to give its readers an objective account of the protection provided by people's homes in the event of a nuclear war. Protection is required against blast, heat and radioactive fallout and the ability of Britain's housing stock to withstand the forces of blast and heat as well as to provide protection against radioactive fallout is examined in detail.

Inevitably, whenever the use of nuclear weapons is discussed, controversy will abound. However, the overriding aim in producing this report is to make available objective findings and to ascertain as exactly as possible what the effects will be for the general public of a 'stay-at-home' civil defence policy.

Other effects of nuclear war, i.e. biological, psychological and economic, are not dealt with here; these have been dealt with elsewhere[1,2,3] and this book is concerned solely with the physical effects of the use of nuclear weapons upon people's homes and other possible forms of shelter.

The method of working involved analysis of all available documentation and recalculation, where appropriate, of damage/casualty figures. Consultation was carried out with various housing agencies, government departments and public service bodies. Questionnaire surveys were carried out concerning the provision of private shelter facilities.

The book is structured in the following way: the remainder of this introduction considers the nature and possibility of nuclear war in the UK. Although later chapters deal with the effects of various levels of attack, the possibility of the UK being involved in a nuclear war is discussed, as well as the most likely form of attack that it could expect.

Chapter 2 deals with the effects of nuclear weapons upon existing residential housing stock in the UK. Residential housing is understood to include the associated service infrastructure of gas, electricity, water supplies and telecommunications. The four specific effects which are considered are: (a) blast; (b) heat and light; (c) radiation; (d) electromagnetic pulse. Chapter 3 deals with the provision of accommodation and services in the UK in the event of a nuclear war and assesses the suitability of existing housing stock for civilian protection. In addition to the 'stay-at-home' civil defence advice given to the general public, additional measures have been taken by the government including the provision of blast-protected shelters. The extent of current civil defence preparations is discussed in order to ascertain what effective help they will be able to provide for the mass of the population sheltering in their homes.

Chapter 4 looks at the ways of increasing the protection afforded by existing structures in the event of a nuclear attack and the cost and effectiveness of so doing. An alternative form of defence for the individual household is the construction of purpose-built protected accommodation (normally in the form of underground shelters). Analysis has been carried out of the various shelters available on the market to ascertain their cost and effectiveness.

Chapter 5 considers the possibilities of reconstructing the physical fabric of the nation's housing stock subsequent to a nuclear attack on either a limited or full scale. Clearly the problems will be less if only one or two bombs are dropped. However, even at this relatively low level of attack, the economic and organisational problems of replacing and repairing several million homes would not be insignificant.

Chapter 6 outlines the conclusions of the investigations carried out in the report and identifies possible courses of action for future governments which would reduce death and destruction of civilians and property in the event of a nuclear attack upon the United Kingdom.

Possibility and Likely Patterns of Nuclear Attack on the UK

Nuclear attack on the UK could range from a limited use of one or two small weapons discharged by way of warning, to a full-scale attack on all major military and civilian targets in the country. Extensive reading of a range of military scenarios for the outbreak of nuclear war (including Gaskell,[4] McMahan[5] and Harries[6]) gives no definite answers except that the likely nature of scale of attack cannot be identified with any certainty. Nevertheless certain patterns of attack are more likely than others.

Before these patterns of attack can be identified, a brief introduction is needed to the types of weapons and warfare at the disposal of the military personnel.

Tactical weapons are those nuclear weapons which are limited to a range of 15 miles and are therefore restricted to battlefield use. These would include low-yield bombs (i.e. like the one dropped on Hiroshima of 12.5 KT), neutron bombs (i.e. enhanced radiation weapons) and nuclear shells fired by artillery. It is unlikely that tactical weapons would be used as part of a land war in the UK. Given the current political situation, the most likely place for such weapons to be used as part of a military conflict would be East and West Germany.

Strategic weapons are those held by the USA and USSR which have the power to threaten the home territory of the other. These weapons can fly between continents in about 20 minutes and include intercontinental ballistic missiles (ICBMs), submarine-launched ballistic missiles (SLBMs), free-fall bombs and air-launched missiles carried by long-range aircraft.

'Theatre' or intermediate-range nuclear weapons represent a group of weapons designed for use between the two above extremes. They are deployed mainly in Europe and include ground-launched cruise missiles. There is no real distinction in either explosive yield or range between strategic and theatre weapons; in fact, theatre weapons, since they are for use mainly in Europe, are sometimes referred to as 'Eurostrategic'. One of the inherent inequalities of the arms race is that both NATO 'strategic' and 'theatre' weapons can reach the home territory of the USSR, whereas only the strategic weapons of the USSR can reach the USA; its theatre weapons can only be used against the USA's European allies.

The US Office of Technology Assessment[7] considers four distinct attack patterns to represent the range of possibilities. These are:

1. An attack against a single city
2. A limited attack, using a specified number of warheads on targets important to the economic activity of the country
3. A counterforce attack on such targets as missiles, bomber bases and submarine bases
4. A full-scale attack, including military, economic and industrial targets, with population not being directly targeted.

Case 3 is considered to be the 'least irrational way of waging nuclear war'.

The trend over the last 20 years of nuclear weapon development has been to increase the accuracy of the weapons. These weapons of greater accuracy have a lower yield and are used for attacking strategic military targets and have contributed to the development of the counterforce strategy as distinct from simple deterrence. This trend continues with the most recently designed weapons having even greater accuracy. A 'counterforce' nuclear attack would be directed against military targets rather than cities as such, and a constant fear is that improvements in weapons technology could one day make a successful first strike possible. Peter Goodwin[8] identifies four factors which now favour first strikes:

1. Satellite radio systems have advanced and now help ships, aircraft and submarines to navigate. If one power attacked without warning it would have the advantage of enjoying good communications with its strategic forces. Also ships, aircraft and submarines can know their positions accurately to enable accurate delivery of missiles.
2. Only VLF (very low frequency) and ELF (extremely low frequency) broadcasts can be used to contact submarines which stay submerged continuously. These depend on the use of extremely large aerials mostly on land which are easily destroyed by missiles; therefore submarines would be isolated from command headquarters except in a first-strike attack.
3. Navigation systems for vessels and aircraft can also be used to guide missiles accurately. After an attack has begun, satellites and ground stations would be among the first targets, so the extra accuracy conferred by peacetime launch conditions would give the attacking side a supreme advantage.
4. Recent improvements in the sonar detection of submarines might eventually make the oceans 'transparent'. Submarines would no longer go undetected so that they, along with missile silos and bomber bases, could join the list of targets in a counterforce war.

The so-called counterforce strategy is now the official policy of the USA and its aim would be the destruction of all known missile bases rather than centres of population.

Likely military and strategic targets for a counterforce attack on the UK have been identified by Campbell[9] and Goodwin[8] and are shown in Figure 1.1. Campbell lists likely targets in the following categories (the number in brackets refers to the number of sites in that category).

1. *Nuclear Strategic Forces*
   (a) Submarines and bases (5)
   (b) Airfields (26)
   (c) Stockpiles (at many of above airfields and 5 major centres)

2. *Command, Control, Communications and Intelligence*
    (a) Strategic command centres (12)
    (b) Other command centres (6)
    (c) Vulnerable communications links (8)
    (d) Other communications links (26)
    (e) Intelligence (16)
3. *Air Defence*
    (a) Missile warning radar (1)
    (b) Long-range radar (13)
    (c) Air defence operations centres (4)
    (d) Air defence missile bases (4)
    (e) Air defence interceptor bases (3)
4. *Industrial*
    (a) Means of nuclear production (including components) (10)
    (b) Means of war production (23)
    (c) Power stations – nuclear (15)
                  – conventional 1,000 MW+ (24)
    (d) Oil and gas terminals and depots (28)
    (e) Chemical industry (11)
5. *Conventional Forces*
    (a) Airfields – military, logistic or dispersal (59)
    (b) Ports – naval or logistic (21)
    (c) Troop concentrations (6)
    (d) Ammunition or material stocks (35)
    (e) Fuel depots – military (7)
    (f) Other logistic (8)
6. *Administration, Industrial and Population*
    (a) Government centres (7)
    (b) Major urban/industrial centres (27)

As can be seen from Figure 1.1, the effects of a counterforce attack on the UK would be virtually identical to that of an all-out attack on centres of population since, on this crowded island, many of the targets lie in or close to areas of population. Clearly the effects of a counterforce attack would be very different for the USA and USSR, where missile silos are situated many hundreds of miles from major centres of population.

Having identified the counterforce attack as the one most likely to be experienced in the UK, it is necessary also to consider the likely scale of the attack as well as the chances of the attack actually occurring at that scale, i.e. the possibilities limiting a nuclear war once it has actually started.

Figure 1.1: Likely Military and Strategic Targets in the Event of a Counterforce Attack

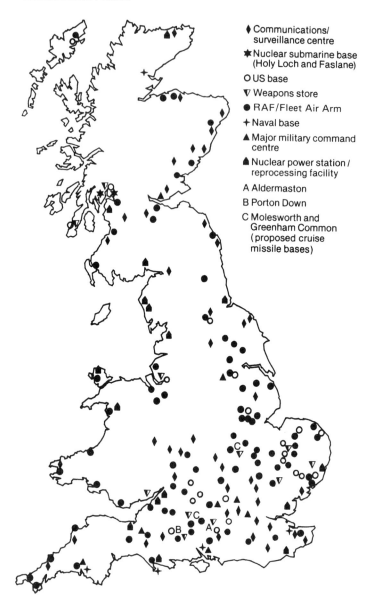

♦ Communications/
   surveillance centre

★ Nuclear submarine base
   (Holy Loch and Faslane)

O US base

▽ Weapons store

● RAF/Fleet Air Arm

+ Naval base

▲ Major military command
   centre

▲ Nuclear power station /
   reprocessing facility

A Aldermaston

B Porton Down

C Molesworth and
   Greenham Common
   (proposed cruise
   missile bases)

Source: LATB Study Group, *London After the Bomb*.

Any attack on the UK would in all probability, given the current political situation, stem from the USSR or its associated Warsaw Pact allies, and would be undertaken with a part of the USSR's 'Eurostrategic' arsenal, delivered by missile and aircraft. The SIPRI Yearbook 1982[14] gives figures for Soviet 'primary Eurostrategic' or longer-range 'theatre' nuclear weapons in 1982. Total yield of warheads (including those likely to be carried by aircraft) exceeds 1,000 megatons.

Many estimates have been made of the scale of a likely attack against the UK,[10,11,12,13] and the broad consensus would seem to be that an attack might amount to 150 megatons to 200 megatons (12,500 times that amount of explosive dropped on Hiroshima) with at least a trebling of this figure if cruise missiles were to be deployed in the UK, since an aggressor would need to bombard the entire area of their deployment (range of 100 miles) in order to ensure the destruction of these missiles.

For the purposes of civil defence 'Square Leg' exercise an attack of 200 megatons on 80 targets was assumed: however in the BMA's report on the medical effects of nuclear war[10] the Home Office is quoted as stating that this figure in no way reflected their assessment of the possible scale of attack from the Soviet Union.

An attack at the level of 200 megatons would be catastrophic for the UK and the only hope of avoiding destruction once the first nuclear weapon has been used (in all probability over German territory), would be that the further use of nuclear weapons could be limited in line with the theory of flexible response. This is the theory which underpins NATO policy in Europe and is that if the scale and nature of attack can be matched at each of a series of levels, so, in theory, can it be deterred. Many experts have derided this concept that nuclear war can be played according to some type of Queensberry Rules for just as a war started with conventional weapons can escalate to the nuclear level, likewise there is a high chance of a tactical nuclear war escalating rapidly to the strategic scale. On the question of war scenarios, SIPRI[15] state that 'on a realistic basis it must be assumed that the worst would happen, once a nuclear war had started'.

In *Nuclear Illusion and Reality*,[16] Professor Zuckerman, former Chief Scientific Adviser to the Ministry of Defence discusses the credibility of 'limited' nuclear war. He states that five out of seven holders of the post of Chief of Defence Staff since 1957 have declared themselves sceptical about the entire idea of limitation. Possibly the most well-known statement is that made by the late Lord Louis Mountbatten, in Strasbourg in May 1979. Lord Mountbatten states: 'I cannot imagine a situation in which nuclear weapons would be used as battlefield weapons without the conflagration spreading . . . I repeat in all sincerity as a military man I can see no use for any nuclear weapons which would not end in escalation, with consequences that no-one can conceive.'

The majority of informed opinion would seem to be against any feasible limitation of the final holocaust once the first bombs have been used.

In oral evidence to the BMA Working Party,[10] however, the Ministry of Defence still appear to argue the rationale of flexible response whereas a spokesman for the Arms Control and Disarmament Research Unit of the Foreign and Commonwealth Office was equivocal about the possibility of a limited nuclear war in Europe on the grounds that 'the Soviet Union has said that any U.S. missile falling on Soviet territory would be treated as coming from the United States and would draw a reaction in response against the United States'.

This fact is made even more frightening by the fact that the first bombs can be delivered accidentally. Stewart Britten in his book entitled *The Invisible Event*[17] assesses the risk of accidental or unauthorised detonation of nuclear weapons and of war by miscalculation. He identifies a variety of causes of 'non-intentional' attack, including accident, miscalculation and unauthorised use. Two main factors lie behind these causes – human failure and pathological motivation (including terrorism). Predisposing causes of disaster are identified as follows:

1. The position of the US President is under increasing stress.
2. Stress exists at lower levels of command, e.g. stress isolation and boredom for ICBM crews – in 1975 and 1976 4 per cent (5,000 people) of US forces on nuclear weapons duties were transferred for drug/alcohol abuse, aberrant behaviour or criminal convictions.
3. Authority in time of crisis is widely spread because of the complexity of the nuclear weaponry system and much of the authority necessarily resides at lower levels of the command structure. All wars create endless opportunities for mistakes and miscalculations.
4. Security problems; new countries acquiring weapons are unlikely at first to have security procedures as stringent as those of present major nuclear nations. Theft of weapons by terrorists is a possibility and annually 0.5 per cent of throughput of fissile material in nuclear power stations is unaccounted for.

A variety of near-misses and accidents have occurred throughout the last 40 years of nuclear weapon development and use. Possibly one of the best known of these occurred in November 1979 when a 'wargame' tape was accidentally fed into a NORAD computer resulting in a live launch of Soviet missiles being indicated. In the six minutes before the error was detected, the strategic nuclear forces were put on a low-level state of 'nuclear war alert'. B52 bombers prepared for take-off and ICBM crews started preliminary launch procedures. In June 1980 failure of an integrated circuit in a computer led to a second false alarm.

Clearly the risks of an accident occurring some day can only increase with the continual proliferation of nuclear weapons throughout the world. However, in addition to the risks of an accident occurring, certain other factors have increased the likelihood of a nuclear war taking place. These include:

1. The increasing advantage of carrying out a first strike (referred to on p. 4). With increasing accuracy of weapons it has become the case that the advantage now lies with the aggressor, whereas previously the aggressor was at a distinct disadvantage.
2. An increasing number of countries have the ability to make nuclear bombs. Britain has a partially independent capability and France and China fully independent capabilities. India has the bomb, Pakistan is thought to be making the first 'Islamic H-bomb'. South Africa and Israel are suspected of having nuclear arsenals and possible starting places for the final holocaust now include Europe, the Sino-Soviet border, the Middle East, South Africa and India/Pakistan.
3. The number of nuclear reactors for the production of electricity is increasing rapidly throughout the world, thus providing the raw materials for nuclear weapons. The technical capability is now widely available. No limitation exists upon this peaceful production of the raw materials for war.

It is obviously impossible to ascertain the exact possibility of nuclear weapons being exploded on UK territory. It would however seem fairly certain that, in view of the factors outlined above, together with the fact that nuclear arsenals are becoming increasingly powerful and accurate, the likelihood of nuclear war is becoming an increasingly real threat to the UK. The chances of war are likewise increased by the increasing advantage of initiating an exchange of nuclear weapons.

In view of the ever-increasing likelihood of nuclear war occurring either by intention or accident, the consideration of civil defence for the UK population must become a high priority for any UK government.

Undeniably the most effective form of civil defence would be global nuclear disarmament; realistically, however, this will not be occurring in the next decade, and simple humanitarian concern, if nothing else, should compel the current UK government to consider the effects of the current civil defence provision. Indications are that the present Conservative government is committed to certain improvements in the existing provision[18] and further discussion of government policy will be found later in this book.

References

1. A.M. Katz, *Life after Nuclear War: The Economic and Social Impacts of Nuclear Attacks on the United States* (Ballinger, Cambridge, Mass., 1982).
2. Medical Campaign against Nuclear Weapons and Medical Association for the Prevention of War, *The Medical Consequences of Nuclear Weapons* (Cambridge, 1981).
3. G. Crossley, *British Civil Defence and Nuclear War: A Critical Assessment with Reference to Economic Consequences*, Peace Research Reports no. 1 (Bradford University School of Peace Studies, 1983).
4. R. Gaskell, *Nuclear Weapons: the Way Ahead* (Menard Press, London, 1981).
5. J. McMahan, *British Nuclear Weapons, For and Against* (Junction Books, London, 1981).
6. R. Harries (ed.), *What Hope in an Armed World?* (Pickering and Inglis Limited, Basingstoke, 1982).
7. Office of Technology Assessment, Congress of the United States, *The Effects of Nuclear War* (Croom Helm, London, 1980).
8. P. Goodwin, *Nuclear War: The Facts on our Survival* (Ash & Grant, London, 1981).
9. D. Campbell, *War Plan U.K.* (Burnett Books, London, 1982).
10. British Medical Association's Board of Science and Education, *The Medical Effects of Nuclear War* (John Wiley & Sons, Chichester, 1983).
11. M. Clarke, *The Nuclear Destruction of Britain* (Croom Helm, London, 1982).
12. J. Peterson (ed.), *AMBIO, A Journal of the Human Environment*, Royal Swedish Academy of Sciences/Pergamon Press, vol. XI, nos. 2-3 (1982).
13. J.K.S. Clayton, *Training Manual for Scientific Advisers*, Scottish Home and Health Department (HMSO, Edinburgh, 1978).
14. Stockholm International Peace Research Institute (SIPRI), *Yearbook 1982: World Armaments and Disarmaments* (Taylor & Francis, London, 1982).
15. Stockholm International Peace Research Institute (SIPRI), *Nuclear Radiation in Warfare* (Taylor & Francis, London, 1981).
16. S. Zuckerman, *Nuclear Illusion and Reality* (Collins, London, 1982).
17. S. Britten, *The Invisible Event* (Menard Press, London, 1983).
18. *The Times*, 21.6.83, p. 1.

2 THE EFFECTS OF A NUCLEAR ATTACK UPON THE UK

> Atomic weapons have changed everything except the way people think.
>
> Albert Einstein

There are four major effects of a nuclear explosion likely to be experienced in the UK. The first three kill and injure people as well as causing damage to physical structures; these are blast, heat and light and ionising radiation. A fourth effect, the electromagnetic pulse, causes no damage to living beings but is capable of widespread destruction of electrical and telecommunications networks. Each effect will be discussed in detail, with particular reference to the damage that would be caused to residential housing and its associated infrastructure.

However, in order that these effects can be more fully understood, a brief introduction is given to the nature of nuclear weapons. A more detailed technical description of the physical reactions involved is set out in Appendix 1.

The most important point to emphasise in describing nuclear weapons is that these are totally different from any other type of weapon that has been used on this earth. Even the two atomic bombs dropped on Japan in 1945 could almost be described as 'pre-nuclear' in view of their small size and crudeness of design and delivery.

How do Nuclear Weapons Work?

Nuclear weapons derive their energy from the process of splitting the atom and they liberate, weight for weight, vastly greater amounts of energy than conventional explosives. Details of exactly how this energy is generated and liberated are set out in Appendix 1. Once the nuclear weapons have been manufactured they are delivered to other targets by means of missiles, bombs or shells and can be fired from silos, submarines, aircraft and even from large guns (NATO's M-110 howitzer guns and the Soviet S23s).

The most important factor in determining the extent of the damage caused by nuclear weapons is their size, i.e. the amount of explosive that they contain. The bomb which destroyed Hiroshima was rated as a

12.5 KT weapon (i.e. equivalent to 12,500 tons of TNT high explosive). Nowadays such small weapons are only designed for battlefield use; weapons held by the USA and USSR are commonly rated in megatons (i.e. millions of tons of TNT high explosive). The SIPRI Yearbook 1980[1] estimated that the total weapons held by the USA comprised 4,000-8,000 MT of explosive yield, those of the USSR 7,000-11,000 MT, the United Kingdom had 200-1,000 MT, China 200-400 MT and France 100 MT, giving a total of between 11,000-20,000 MT of explosive yield in the world. One of the largest known bombs ever to have been exploded experimentally was rated at 57 MT, although this would involve such massive overkill as to be a waste of explosive. Much greater damage can be achieved by using a larger number of smaller-yield weapons.

Table 2.1 shows how the blast and heats effects vary according to the size of the weapon.

Table 2.1: Effects of Different Size Nuclear Weapons (Range in Miles)

Effect	Weapon Size				
	1 KT	150 KT	1 MT	10 MT	20 MT
Range of lethal initial radiation	0.5	1.2	1.6	2.5	3.0
Range for skin reddening	0.5	5.5	10.0	24.0	30.0
Range for charred skin	0.4	3.5	8.0	18.0	23.0
Range for fatal wind drag (human dragged at 40 ft/sec)	0.2	1.6	3.3	8.0	10.0
Range of devastation for building above ground (12 p.s.i.)	0.3	1.3	2.5	5.0	7.0
Range of severe blast damage (4 p.s.i.)	0.5	2.6	5.0	11.0	13.0
Range at which all windows broken (1 p.s.i.)	1.3	7.0	13.0	28.0	36.0
assuming air-burst at optimum height					

Source: P. Goodwin, *Nuclear Weapons: the Facts on our Survival*.

There is no simple link between range of effects and weapon size (i.e. the blastwave from a 10 MT bomb does not extend ten times as far as that from a 1 MT bomb). Scaling laws have been devised to estimate the ranges at which specific effects will result from nuclear weapons of different powers. The HMSO publication *Nuclear Weapons*[2] explains this 'cube-root' law of weapon power as follows:

The power of a nuclear weapon is defined as the total energy released in detonation. Thus, a 10 MT bomb is 500 times as powerful as a

20 KT bomb and so liberates 500 times as much energy in each of the forms of radiation, blast and fission products. Now the cube root of 500 ($\sqrt[3]{500}$) is nearly 8 and it has been found that the two weapons produce the same peak pressure (blast intensity) at distances from ground zero which differ by a factor of 8. In other words, the peak pressure at, say, 1 mile from the 20 KT detonation will be the same as the peak pressure, at $1 \times \sqrt[3]{500}$ of 8 miles from the 10 MT detonation.

The effects produced by the detonation of a nuclear weapon can also vary considerably depending on the height at which it is exploded. Weapons may burst: (i) on or near the ground; (ii) in shallow or deep water; (iii) high in the air; (iv) very high, on the fringe of the earth's atmosphere.

The effects of these different types of weapon burst are described in detail in the HMSO publication *Nuclear Weapons*[2] and are summarised below.

Ground Bursts (bomb detonated on ground or at such a low level that the fireball touches the surface beneath it)

— Explosion generates a fireball, as hot as the sun, which shoots upward, carrying with it much vaporised soil material
— Partial vacuum left behind as fireball rises causing a strong wind (at 200 mph+) to move onwards and upwards, carrying dust and debris
— Debris falls back to earth covered with radioactive particles, larger pieces falling near the crater, smaller pieces (less than 2 mm) being carried by the wind

The large quantities of energy released are distributed in the following form (at or near ground level)

Form of Energy	% of Total Energy Released
Blast and shock waves	45
Light and heat radiation	35
Initial nuclear radiation	5
Residual radiation from fission products (fallout)	15

In a ground burst, an appreciable amount of energy is used up in forming the crater and some of the initial heat and nuclear radiations will be absorbed by the crater material. Ranges of blast, fires and skin burns will be less than from an air burst of the same power.

Water Bursts

In shallow water — large amounts of water and bottom mud carried up into fireball
— at high altitude vaporised water is condensed to rain and brings down radioactive fission products
— fallout is less extensive but more intensive than for ground burst
— wet fallout is more difficult to remove

In deep water — similar to above (without the mud) except that larger amounts of total energy released will be used in producing a shockwave through water forming surface waves and in vaporising water.

Bursts of this type have little military value.

Air Bursts (detonated so that fireball is well clear of the surface beneath it)

— A very few dust particles for fission products to stick to and so, as minute particles, they will be dispersed far and wide before reaching the ground. Fallout is therefore a far less significant hazard with air bursts. Hazardous fallout is possible, however, in the event of rain falling through the cloud.
— Range of blast and fire damage is greater than for ground bursts since energy is not dissipated in the formation of a crater.

High-altitude Bursts

— At more than 100,000 feet (30 km) an explosion is termed a high-altitude explosion, since it is above most of the earth's atmosphere
— At this height the major effect is damage over a wide area (radius of several thousand miles) to electrical components, e.g. it can burn out transistors, destroy shortwave radio and computer systems and cause disruptive instabilities in power grids
— This damage is caused by a single very high voltage pulse known as the electromagnetic pulse (EMP) which lasts for a very short time

The effects of the nuclear weapon will depend on other factors as well as weapon size and height of burst. Topography, climate, time of day and year will also affect the amount of damage caused.

Topography will play an important part in determining the effects of

Table 2.2: Extent of Main Fire Zone, Range in Miles

Visibility (miles)	20 KT		500 KT		1 MT		5 MT		10 MT	
	Surface	Air	Surface	Air	Surface	Air	Surface	Air	Surface	Air
2	3/8 – ¾	½ – 1¼	1¼ – 2½	1½ – 4	1½ – 3	1¾ – 5	2¾ – 5	3¼ – 8½	3½ – 5½	4 – 10
8	3/8 – 7/8	½ – 13/8	1¼ – 3	1½ – 5	1½ – 4	1¾ – 6½	2¾ – 7	3¼ – 12	3½ – 9	4 – 15
32	3/8 – 1	7/8 – 3	1¼ – 3½	1½ – 6	1½ – 5	1¾ – 8	2¾ – 9	3¼ – 15	3½ – 12	4 – 20

Weapon Size and Burst

the blast and heat waves since a hilly landscape will provide a shielding effect and also make it less likely that a fire-storm could develop. This was clearly seen in Japan, where damage at Hiroshima, which lay on a flat plain, was much more extensive than that at Nagasaki, where a series of hills near the centre of the town provided relative protection for at least some of the population. In addition, although there were extensive fires in Nagasaki, there was not the terrible fire-storm that developed in Hiroshima and this is widely attributed to the differences in the topography of the two towns.

The meteorological conditions are also extremely important, as will be described later in detail. The range of the heat effects depends very much on the prevailing visibility as Table 2.2 shows. If there is heavy cloudcover between the burst weapon and the earth, then much of the thermal radiation (heat and light) will be reflected away from the earth. The meteorological conditions will also determine the shape, extent and location of the fallout pattern. The windspeed and direction will largely determine where local fallout will occur; if it is raining then the fallout will occur more rapidly than otherwise. Also the climate will affect the number of people likely to be out of doors at any particular time.

The time of day and time of year are also important. These two factors have little effect on the number of buildings damaged or the extent of that damage, but they have great importance with regard to the number of people killed or injured.

The time of day that the bomb is dropped will influence where people are. Bombs dropped at night will cause few direct skin-burns and little flash-blindness, since most people will be asleep in bed; there may however be a greater incidence of people being trapped, crushed or burned in their homes. Bombs dropped in the day over cities will kill more people since daytime populations are enlarged by commuting workers. The time of year will also determine whether or not people are in or out of doors, whether they have layers of clothing on or wear only very light clothing.

Clearly, therefore, the effects of nuclear weapons are not standard and will vary according to a whole range of conditions; general guidelines have long been documented[3,4] as to the likely effects of the usage of different size weapons and it is these general effects that are to be discussed below.

What Happens when a Nuclear Weapon is Exploded?

Once a nuclear weapon has been exploded, a fireball (which is as hot as the sun) is created. In less than a thousandth of a second after detonation the fireball from a 1 MT explosion grows to more than 100 metres wide and after ten seconds is nearly 2 kilometres wide.[3] At the same time it rises at a rate of approximately 100 metres every second. If the fireball touches the ground, soil and other materials are vaporised and taken up with the fireball. Immediately after the detonation a short flash of light is emitted of an intensity sufficient temporarily to blind anyone looking towards it. The tremendous heat from the fireball travels at almost the speed of light in a direct line away from the fireball. Readily ignitable materials that are exposed and in its direct path will flare up or be charred. Exposed skin will also be burned. At the instant of the explosion intense initial radiation is given off; this has a very limited range, however, and anyone near enough to receive this will be killed instantaneously by the other effects of the explosion. The blastwave generated by the explosion spreads out in all directions; travelling at the speed of sound it arrives after the heatwave has passed. The blastwave from a 1 MT bomb takes approximately 15 seconds to extend 6 kilometres from the source of the explosion and it is accompanied by winds blowing at hundreds of miles per hour. This blastwave can also cause fires where the heatwave may not have done; for example by wrecking stoves, furnaces and gas mains, bringing down power lines and destroying gas and oil stores.

An hour or so after the explosion the fallout particles created at the moment of explosion and sucked up into the fireball begin to return to earth, carrying radioactive fission products. They are carried by the wind and come down from the atmosphere in an unpredictable way, differing according to local variations in land relief, wind, clouds and rain. These particles continue to emit radiation where they fall but the intensity of the radioactivity is progressively reduced over the following weeks and months until it is too weak to damage human tissue.

The standard authority on the effects of nuclear weapon is Glasstone and Dolan, *The Effects of Nuclear Weapons*,[3] which is widely acknowledged as an accurate and definitive work on weapons effects: most of the world's bodies concerned with civil defence, including the United Kingdom government, have used it as a reliable source of data. It is issued by the Home Office to its regional scientific advisers and is used in the Home Office. It is likewise used here as the major source for calculations of weapons effects.

There are four major effects of the use of nuclear weapons and these are set out below. It is vitally important to remember that, in reality, these effects will occur almost simultaneously in overlapping spatial patterns and that total damage would far exceed the sum of the parts.

The Effect of Blast upon Residential Housing

At the moment of explosion of a nuclear weapon, enormous pressure builds up within a fraction of a second and this is the source of the high-pressure blastwave which is transmitted outwards through the air. Approximately one half of the total energy of the weapon is in the form of a blastwave; the front of this wave spreads in all directions with a speed several times greater than the speed of sound. As it progresses the wave loses speed and amplitude.

The blast of a nuclear explosion produces two types of damaging effect:

1. Sudden increases in air pressure which are strong enough to crush objects. This is known as 'static overpressure' and is measured as the amount by which the air pressure exceeds normal air pressure (14.7 pounds per square inch (p.s.i.)).
2. High winds, known as 'dynamic overpressure', which can move objects and knock them down. These winds range in speed according to the size of the weapon, whether air or ground burst, and they decline in speed the further they travel from the point of explosion. For example, for a 1 MT air-burst weapon, wind speeds for the first mile from ground zero are 1,700 m.p.h. falling to 400 m.p.h. at 2 miles, 130 m.p.h. at 5 miles and 50 m.p.h. at 10 miles.

In general, large buildings are destroyed by the static overpressure, while people and objects (trees, telegraph poles, aerials, etc.) are destroyed by the winds. Even those inside buildings can be killed by flying glass and debris and winds associated with an overpressure as little as 2-3 p.s.i. can be expected to blow people out of typical modern office buildings.[4]

However, as Tucker and Gleisner[5] point out, it is misleading to interpret the blast effects of nuclear weapons in the light of experience of conventional explosives. The pressure waves associated with nuclear weapons produce much larger stress on structures than conventional explosives of the same energy. In addition, the acceleration period for materials carried by the blastwaves are longer and the speeds of objects caught in the blast are higher than in comparable conventional blast situations. Thus, for the same apparent overpressure zone, the hazards of a nuclear burst, from blast alone, are greater than from conventional bursts.

Peter Goodwin[6] identifies several ways in which the blastwave could destroy buildings. First, total blast overpressure can simply squash a building flat. Overpressure of 5 p.s.i. (as shown in Table 2.3, a peak overpressure of 5 p.s.i. will extend up to 4.4 miles from ground zero of a 1 MT air-burst weapon), would be enough to destroy most buildings in the United Kingdom. Secondly, if the building had few windows and doors open, it might simply be crushed flat because external pressure is much greater than that inside. Thirdly, if those sides and roof not facing the blastwave were strong enough, they might withstand the maximum overpressure but the side facing the blast would be under greater pressure and would in all probability collapse, bringing the remainder of the building with it. Fourthly, since the blastwave from the larger bombs can take several seconds to pass completely, in any building with doors and windows open (or blasted out by a previous bomb), the extra pressure would force air into the building and as soon as the wave had passed it would explode. For example, ten miles away from a 10 MT explosion the blast overpressure of 4 p.s.i. would take about 8 seconds to pass, and whilst the overpressure of 4 p.s.i. wouldn't flatten most buildings, the tremendous pressure built up in the 8 seconds would cause most buildings that remained standing to explode.

A further way in which the blastwave can destroy buildings is by causing fires to start. This would commonly occur when the blastwave knocked over stoves and other sources of open flame in the home, by rupturing gas mains and damaging petrol depots and stations; by bringing down electricity cables and by starting electrical fires.

Unlike thermal radiation (described in detail later), the blastwave kills very few people directly, since overpressures of up to 30 p.s.i. are not lethal on their own. However, a person would need to be very near to ground zero to experience overpressure of more than 30 p.s.i. and at this distance would certainly be killed by any variety of weapons effects. The blastwave, however, can kill indirectly as a result of people being caught in collapsing buildings or being struck by falling or flying objects.

Extent of Blastwave Damage

The amount and extent of the damage caused by the blastwave depends both on the power of the weapon and the height at which it is exploded.

If the weapon were exploded at ground level it would produce very large overpressures over very short distances; such bursts would be used to destroy very hard targets such as missile silos. If the weapon were air-burst, however, it would not produce such high overpressures but the effects of the blastwave would be spread over much larger areas.

As mentioned earlier, the range of blast effects of a nuclear explosion is not directly proportional to yield but only to the cube root of the yield. Thus an 8 MT bomb would be needed to extend a given level of overpressure to twice the extent of a 1 MT bomb.

The usual method of describing the extent of blast damage around a nuclear explosion is to denote a series of concentric circles around the point of explosion corresponding to the different levels of overpressure and damage caused. Although this analogy is used below, it must be remembered that in practice the shapes of hills and valleys could substantially modify these effects, as indeed was the case at Nagasaki.

The Home Office have designated four concentric rings (denoted Rings A, B, C and D) to describe the blast effects.[2,7] These are as follows: A Ring has an overpressure of 11 p.s.i. and over and houses are totally destroyed in this ring; B Ring has overpressure of 6-11 p.s.i. and houses are irreparably damaged in this ring; the C Ring has overpressure of 1.5-6 p.s.i. and houses suffer moderate to severe damage; finally, D Ring has overpressure of 0.75-1.5 p.s.i., and houses here are only lightly damaged.

Houses in the A Ring of total destruction would be reduced entirely to rubble with an occasional wall partially standing. Houses in the B Ring would be standing, albeit with severe cracks in masonry. The roof would be completely destroyed, likewise all doors and windows and interior fittings. Damage in the C Ring would be so severe that repairs would not be possible under conventional, let alone nuclear, war conditions. Doors and windows would be blown out, there would be large holes in the roof and cracked masonry but virtually all houses would still be standing. The light damage experienced in D Ring would normally include extensive loosening of tiles on the roof, broken windows, damaged interior fittings. Little structural damage occurs in this ring. Minor repairs only would be needed before houses would be habitable again. The problem of debris, rubble and glass covering the streets will occur in all areas, however, and will present a great problem in reaching buildings either to put out fires or rescue occupants.

The problems of radioactive fallout in the days following the explosion will also prevent many people being rescued from collapsed buildings who could otherwise have been dug out. The experience of the blastwave from a nuclear bomb is therefore far removed from that of Second World War bombing raids, where relatively few of the civil population sheltering in their homes actually died, even though their homes may have been badly damaged.

Since the modern high-rise block commonly found in many of our cities today was not present at the time of Japanese bombing there is no available evidence as to how such buildings would withstand the blastwave effects. Possibly the only comparison with the Japanese experience is with the reinforced concrete frame office-type buildings of 3-10 storeys with lightweight low-strength walls of non-earthquake-resistant construction (since Hiroshima lay in an earthquake zone many of the buildings were designed to be earthquake resistant). Here, after the dropping of the very small nuclear weapon the damage was as follows:

Area of Severe Damage	— Severe frame distortion, incipient collapse
Area of Moderate Damage	— Frame distorted moderately, interior partitions blown down, some spalling of concrete
Area of Light Damage	— Windows and doors blown in, light siding ripped off, interior partitions cracked

Source: Glasstone and Dolan, *The Effects of Nuclear Weapons*.

Clearly therefore extensive damage would be suffered by even medium-height high-rise blocks, with the additional problem for the occupants of how to reach the comparative safety of the ground floor.

The figures put forward by the Home Office as to the extent of these different Rings have however been seriously called into question, as described in detail below, and therefore, as an example of their extent for a 1 MT air burst, figures produced by Glasstone and Dolan[3] are used in Table 2.3, rather than those by the Home Office.

The Office of Technology Assessment of the United States[4] has also produced figures covering damage to a wider range of structures than houses and these are set out in Table 2.4 to indicate further the likely landscape that could be expected after the explosion of a 1 MT nuclear weapon.

Figures for the extent of blast effects for different size weapons were given earlier in this chapter in Table 2.1.

The only sources of information which can be used to calculate the extent of the blast effects reliably are observed data from the Hiroshima and Nagasaki bombs and from above-ground nuclear weapons tests conducted before the partial nuclear test ban treaty in 1963. There is substantial agreement between the Japanese and American findings[8,4] as to expected blast casualties. Home Office figures, however, are substantially lower and in *London After the Bomb*[9] the two reasons put forward for this are that the Home Office assumes that high blast pressures are confined to smaller areas than those given by American sources and that for a given level of blast, the Home Office expects a smaller proportion of people to be killed or injured. These Home Office estimates are widely regarded as underestimates, since the American sources, especially that of Glasstone and Dolan as stated earlier, are widely recognised as the standard authority on the subject.

Table 2.3: Blast Effects for a 1 MT Air-burst Weapon (range in kilometres)

Ring Designation	Overpressure	Radius of Damage Zone	Likely Damage to Houses
A	11 p.s.i. +	4.25 km (2.65 miles)	Total destruction
B	6 – 11 p.s.i.	6.0 km (3.75 miles)	Irreparably damaged
C	1.5 – 6 p.s.i.	14.5 km (9.1 miles)	Moderate to severe damage
D	0.75 – 1.5 p.s.i.	24.0 km (15 miles)	Light damage

Table 2.4: Blast Effects for 1 MT Air-burst Weapon on a Variety of Structures

Peak Overpressure (p.s.i.)	Radius of Damage Zone (km)	Typical Blast Effects
20	1.3 (0.8 miles)	Reinforced concrete structures are levelled
10	4.8 (3.0 miles)	Most factories and commercial buildings are collapsed. Small wood-frame and brick residences destroyed and distributed as debris
5	7.0 (4.4 miles)	Lightly constructed commercial buildings and typical residences are destroyed; heavier construction is severely damaged
3	9.5 (5.9 miles)	Walls of typical steel-frame buildings are blown away; severe damage to residences. Winds sufficient to kill people in the open
1	18.6 (11.6 miles)	Damage to structures; people endangered by flying glass and debris

Source: Office of Technology Assessment, *The Effects of Nuclear War*.

Table 2.5: Radius of Damage Zones for Different Peak Overpressures – for 1 MT Air-burst and Ground-burst Weapons

| Peak Overpressure | 1 MT Ground Burst | | | | 1 MT Air Burst | | | |
| | Radius of Damage Zone (km) | | Area of Damage Zone (km²) | | Radius of Damage Zone (km) | | Area of Damage Zone (km²) | |
	Home Office	Glasstone	Home Office	Glasstone	Home Office	Glasstone	Home Office	Glasstone
11 (Ring A)	2.5	3.0	19.6	28.2	3.25	4.25	33.1	56.7
6 (Ring B)	3.5	4.0	38.5	50.2	4.55	6.0	65.0	113.0
1.5 (Ring C)	9.0	9.0	254.3	254.3	11.7	14.5	429.8	660.18
0.75 (Ring D)	14.0	14.0	615.4	615.4	18.2	24.0	1040.1	1808.6

Source: BMA Report, *The Medical Effects of Nuclear War.*

The British Medical Association[10] have highlighted the differences in official estimates as produced by the American authorities and the UK Home Office. These are summarised and set out in Table 2.5. The BMA Report states that the Home Office agreed in evidence to its Working Party that these differences exist but said that 'It is not possible to discuss in every case which is "correct", as the range for a given over-pressure may be influenced by a number of factors.' The discrepancies in the radii of damage rings are noticeably greater for air bursts than for surface bursts and these discrepancies are naturally enhanced when the area of the damage zone rather than the radius is considered; for instance, under Home Office calculations for 1 MT air-burst weapon, a total of 98.1 square kilometres would be damaged in Rings A and B, whereas under Glasstone and Dolan's figures this would be 113.0 square kilometres.

There are likewise considerable discrepancies in the estimated blast casualty rates, with Home Office figures being much lower than those produced by the American sources. Human casualties are however not the primary concern of this book and these casualty rates are therefore not discussed here in detail.

Blastwave Damage to Service Infrastructure

In addition to the damage that it can cause to the houses themselves, the blastwave can also cause considerable damage to the services supplied to those houses, i.e. water, gas, electricity. The extent of the damage will depend largely upon the size of weapon exploded and whether it was air or ground burst.

When a nuclear weapon is exploded at or near ground level, much of the energy is expended in forming the crater. At the same time a shock-wave is transmitted outwards through the ground. Clearly any under-ground or overground conduits or cables in the crater area will be completely destroyed; in addition, however, the ground shockwave also causes damage to underground service lines and connections. Any ground shock effects above ground are only within that area destroyed by the blastwave and are thus irrelevant. The Home Office[7] notes that the extent of the damage depends on: (i) duration of the blastwave (i.e. power of weapon); (ii) type of soil; (iii) moisture content of soil; (iv) depth of structure below ground; (v) shape of the structure. The longer the blastwave takes to pass, the greater the damage that will be caused. The ground shockwave from a 1 MT weapon can be compared to an earthquake of moderate intensity where the greater the vibration that is experienced the greater the damage. The more compact and dry the soil the greater the resistance offered to the shockwave, dry rock being the most resistant of mediums. The deeper the structure is below ground, the less will be the impact of the shock wave. Flexible structures such as pipes usually adjust to some degree of ground movement and small self-contained structures will generally move bodily with the earth movement.

In addition to the ground shock associated with the ground-burst weapon, the blastwave travelling above the ground will destroy many of the pylons or other support poles in addition to processing plant, e.g. pumping stations, electricity substations.

In the case of an air-burst weapon, the ground shock effects will not be so pronounced as for the ground-burst weapon but damage above ground will extend further for a given weapon yield, as explained earlier.

Damage to Water Supply

In the Home Office circular *Water Services in War*[11] the government states that 'It can be said with absolute assurance that any widespread nuclear attack would quickly disrupt the distribution system for domestic and industrial water . . . Outside the areas of total destruction close to the burst of the weapon, particularly vulnerable elements of many systems are water towers, surface reservoirs and pumping stations.'

Whilst the blastwave is unlikely to damage underground pipes which are usually designed to resist earth tremors, a likely source of damage to the piped supply is where it emerges into the house and could be ruptured through blast or fire damage. However, as stated by I. Tyrell,[12] although it is probable that the water mains will survive intact in most areas, water towers, reservoirs and pumping stations are more vulnerable to the effects of nuclear weapons (and need constant electricity or fuel supplies) — and therefore although the distribution system remains unharmed, there will be no safe water to pass through it. Blast damage to pumping stations, water towers, etc. would need to be repaired before any piped supply could be recommenced.

Damage to Electricity Supply

As with the water supply, the supply of electricity to homes is dependent on a linked chain from generating stations (which need to be fuelled) through switching stations and substations via both overhead and underground cables. A failure in any one part will automatically stop supply. The blastwave and fire effects would destroy much of the national grid and some of the power stations. Since electricity generating stations are widely dispersed it is unlikely that they will all sustain blast damage and it is damage to the national grid itself that is likely to prove more extensive and crippling. Pylons and poles are especially sensitive to the drag effects of the blastwave, although due to the fact that many of the electricity cables in the built-up areas of the UK are underground, damage will be less extensive than in those countries where there is widescale overhead carriage. Of the 222 power stations in Britain, the 20 nuclear power stations and the 25 conventional power stations which produce between 1 and 2 GW per annum would be likely counterforce targets themselves. Electricity supply will fail virtually immediately in the event of a nuclear attack and reconnection of the domestic consumer will be the lowest priority in time of reconstruction.

Damage to Gas Supply

Again, since the bulk of gas distribution in the UK is underground, the network of buried pipes is likely to survive largely intact except in the areas of total destruction. However, gas distribution equipment and storage installations would be liable to blast damage, especially since these are to be found virtually exclusively in built-up areas. There would be fractured pipes and consequent leaks near bomb bursts with the heatwave bringing the likelihood of explosions.

Natural gas pipelines from the North Sea come ashore at just four points in the UK – St Furgus (Scotland), Easington, Theddlethorpe and Bacton. These would therefore be likely targets themselves and if destroyed the entire UK natural gas supply network would cease to operate.

The Effects of Thermal Radiation upon Residential Housing

As outlined earlier, 35 per cent of the energy of a nuclear weapon is given off as thermal radiation, i.e. heat and light. This is one of the major differences between nuclear and conventional high explosive weapons since this massive release of intense thermal radiation does not occur with conventional weapons.

The thermal radiation is given off in two distinct pulses, both occurring within seconds of the explosion of the bomb. The first pulse carries only a very small percentage of the total energy and is seen as brilliant light. It comprises mainly ultraviolet radiation and can cause temporary blindness to anyone looking directly at its source. This first pulse has no effect on built structures. The second pulse carries the vast proportion of the energy and is felt as heat which can cause severe burns and start fires over a large area. It was the ability of this heatwave to cause spontaneous ignition that was responsible for much of the damage and loss of life experienced in Hiroshima and Nagasaki. The blastwave, travelling at less than the speed of light, arrives seconds after the heatwave has passed.

Thermal radiation causes damage in two major ways: first, by scorching, charring or causing spontaneous ignition of combustible materials; and secondly, in conjunction with the blastwave, it can be instrumental in causing mass fires.

Unless it has been scattered in a dense atmosphere, thermal radiation travels in a straight line from the fireball. Any solid, opaque material such as a building, a hill or a tree will shield a given object or person and provide protection. If, however, scattering has occurred, the thermal radiation is likely to arrive from all angles and little protection will be available by simple shielding. The thermal radiation emitted by a nuclear weapon is not only of a very high temperature (thousands of degrees centigrade), it is also emitted in a very short time and it therefore has the ability at short distances to vaporise people and metals. Temperatures fall off rapidly with distance, however, and more commonly found effects are burning of the skin (which can easily be fatal without prompt medical attention) and scorching, charring and possibly igniting of combustible materials such as wood, fabric and paper. Thin or porous materials are more likely to flame when exposed than thicker, denser materials. Likewise dark-coloured fabrics will absorb more radiation and burn more easily than lighter colours; man-made fabrics will melt rather than char or burn.

The extent and type of damage caused by the heatwave will vary according to several factors:

Size of the Weapon. The greater the explosive power of the weapon used, the more far-reaching will be the heatwave. This is shown in Table 2.6.

Height of the Explosion. If the weapon is ground burst, much of the heat energy is absorbed by the dust from the crater and surrounding earth, and by shielding from irregular terrain and buildings. If the weapon is air burst there are far fewer obstacles to the movement of the heatwave. Glasstone and Dolan[3] estimate that the amount of thermal energy reaching a specified distance from a ground burst is only 50-75 per cent of that from an air burst. In subsurface bursts nearly all the thermal radiation is absorbed.

Table 2.6: Heat Effects of an Air-burst Weapon*

| Effect | 1 KT | Weapon Size | | | |
		150 KT	1 MT	10 MT	20 MT
Range for skin reddening (miles)	0.5	5.5	10	24	30
Range for charred skin (miles)	0.4	3.5	8	18	23
Range for 2% of buildings gutted by fire (2 p.s.i. blast) (miles)	0.8	4.2	8	17	22
Range for 10% of buildings gutted by fire (5 p.s.i. blast) (miles)	0.4	2.2	4.3	9.3	12

*Assuming burst at optimum height.
Source: P. Goodwin, *Nuclear War: the Facts on our Survival*.

Atmospheric Conditions. Atmospheric conditions form the major limitation to the movement (through the atmosphere) of the heatwave from an air-burst weapon. If the air burst occurs above a layer of dense cloud, smoke or fog there will be a substantial reduction in the amount of thermal radiation reaching a ground target. If the air burst occurs beneath a layer of cloud, however, it is likely that the heat effects will be increased, since little of the heat will be lost to the atmosphere.

The extent to which the various heat effects of different size weapons are experienced is set out in Table 2.7. The actual effects at ground level of the heatwave will vary according to several factors, including those outlined above, as well as local shielding and topographical effects: the figures in Table 2.7 therefore should be regarded only as an approximate guide to the likely scale of damage.

As stated earlier, thermal radiation causes damage in two major ways. The direct heat effects have been outlined above; the second major cause of damage is the interaction of blast and fire which can cause the spread of fires in built-up areas and even, under certain conditions, the creation of mass fires.

Glasstone and Dolan[3] outline in detail the various conditions which affect the spread of fires in cities. These include weather, terrain, closeness and combustibility of buildings and the amount of combustible material in a given area. Fires can spread between buildings in several ways: (a) spontaneous ignition of combustible materials by heat from fires in adjacent buildings; (b) ignition of heated combustible materials by contact with flames, sparks, embers or burning brands;

(c) ignition of unheated combustible materials by flames or burning brands.

Table 2.7: Heat Effects at Different Distances (miles) from Ground Zero for Different Size Weapons*

	Weapon Size			
Effect	20 KT	500 KT	1 MT	10 MT
Most substances incl. metals vaporise	0 — 0.3	0 — 1.5	0 — 2.2	0 — 8
Metal melts	0.25 — 0.5	1.2 — 2.6	1.8 — 3.5	5.2 — 10.1
Rubber and plastics melt and ignite	0.5 — 1.0	2.5 — 4.4	3.4 — 7.1	9.9 — 20.1
Wood chars and burns	0.7 — 1.1	3.4 — 5.4	4.9 — 8.1	14.1 — 23.2
3rd degree burns (charred skin), paper and fabrics ignite	1.2 — 2.1	5.5 — 10.4	8.3 — 14.5	24.5 — 45.4
2nd degree burns (blistering)	1.7 — 3.0	8.5 — 16.0	10.7 — 21.0	33.0 — 75.0
1st degree burns (reddens skin)	1.9 — 3.8	8.8 — 18.5	11.8 — 25.0	51.0 — 80.0

*Due to the many factors affecting the likely effects of the heatwave these figures should only be regarded as approximate.

An important factor determining the probable extent of damage in the distance between buildings; the lower the density, the less chance there is that fire will spread. However, where substantial blast damage has occurred, a continuous layer of debris would provide increased opportunity for the spread of fires. Clearly windspeed and direction will play an important role in determining the final amount of damage done, as will local topography, since hills provide a shield against blast and heat effects. Despite study of Second World War incendiary bombing and nuclear weapon usage in Japan, detailed conditions under which fires spread and mass fires develop are still not known with any certainty.

Mass fires have a great potential for destruction, and indeed, as will be seen in the next section, it was the incidence of mass fires in Hiroshima and Nagasaki that caused much of the extensive damage there. Mass fires are created when individual fires coalesce into either fire-storms or conflagrations. In a fire-storm high winds are generated and are drawn into the centre of the fire area and help fuel the flames. These in-rushing winds prevent the spread of fires outwards but also mean that everything in the affected area is destroyed. Several square miles of old Hamburg were destroyed and over 130,000 people in Dresden were killed in the fire-storms which occurred there subsequent to incendiary attacks in the Second World War. Even in shelters specially designed for protection against nuclear weapons, the occupants may perish through asphyxiation if they are within the area of the fire-storm, since the fire-storm will draw out the oxygen from the shelter to fuel the fire; carbon monoxide will be produced which is lethal for human beings.

Whereas a fire-storm is likely to kill a high proportion of those trapped within it, either through burning or asphyxiation, a conflagration spreads more slowly, thus affording people in its path a greater opportunity to escape. Conflagrations have moving fire-fronts which are driven by the ambient wind and they continue to spread so long as there is sufficient fuel to maintain them. They are thus capable of devastating regions far removed from other weapons effects.

The Home Office[2] dismisses the likelihood of fire-storms occurring in British cities on the grounds that: (a) shielding would prevent a large number of buildings from exposure to the heat flash; (b) buildings are more widely spaced than 30-40 years ago; (c) more buildings are of fire-resistant construction today than ever before.

If spaces between buildings are greater, however, it would seem unwise to rely too greatly on the effect of shielding. Although buildings are more fire resistant in design today, it is also a fact that a much higher proportion of a building is given over to glazing. Many office buildings in particular have their outside walls comprising over 80 per cent glass. Windows are the major means by which thermal radiation enters buildings, and thus modern design increases the risk of individual and mass fires. Likewise, modern furniture and fittings have known propensities to create poisonous fumes in addition to rapid flaring. Flexible polyurethane foam is widely used in modern upholstery, and was found in tests and observations done by the Building Research Establishment[13,14] to be easily flammable and to give off toxic fumes. Fires were shown to develop much more rapidly in modern upholstered furniture than in more traditionally upholstered furniture and to proceed especially rapidly once the flaming stage is reached. Heat flash passing through larger windows and causing spontaneous ignition of highly combustible material would seem to be in fact more conducive to the creation of individual fires and thus mass fires than the Home Office reasoning would indicate.

However, as stated above, the likelihood of the creation of mass fires using the larger nuclear weapons (i.e. 1 MT and over) is not known with any degree of certainty and cannot be ascertained by experiment. Experience gained in the Second World War, whilst indicating likely conditions for the creation of fire-storms using conventional explosives on housing of differing design and construction, cannot be reliably extrapolated to indicate likely results of using nuclear weapons on modern house design. Experience in Hiroshima, where there was a fire-storm, and in Nagasaki, where there was a conflagration, is the only real indicator of likely outcomes and even these observations are limited by the extremely small size of the weapons used.

There is therefore a very strong possibility that, with the use of megaton weapons, such mass fires could develop and it would seem unwise to ignore this possibility in civil defence planning.

Thermal Radiation Effects at Hiroshima and Nagasaki

Probably the most informative evidence as to the heat effects of nuclear weapon usage can be obtained by looking at what happened in Hiroshima and Nagasaki where nuclear weapons, albeit very small ones, were dropped on existing cities.

The effects of the heatwaves at Hiroshima and Nagasaki are well documented,[8,3] many of the major points being summarised in the BMA Report.[10]

The heat experienced at Nagasaki where a 22 KT bomb was exploded (as opposed to the 12.5 KT bomb at Hiroshima) was twice that at Hiroshima. Even at Hiroshima, however, the thermal radiation received in the first three seconds at a distance of 500 metres from ground zero was still 600 times as great as the sun on a bright day, and at a distance of 3 kilometres was still 40 times more than that from the sun. The heat was sufficient to burn exposed human skin at distances up to 4 km from ground zero. Many people caught in the open within 1.2 km of ground zero were burnt to death or vaporised.

Two-thirds of the 76,000 buildings in Hiroshima were destroyed by fire; 25 per cent of Nagasaki's 51,000 buildings were totally destroyed and many more seriously damaged. Nagasaki suffered less damage because of a difference in terrain and building density. Hiroshima was relatively flat and highly built up, whereas Nagasaki had hilly portions near ground zero that were bare of structures. A total of 13 square kilometres in Hiroshima and 7 square kilometres in Nagasaki was reduced to ashes by fire, the higher figure for Hiroshima being due to the fact that a fire-storm developed here, unlike Nagasaki, where topographical features prevented the development of a fire-storm, although a conflagration caused extensive damage.

There was extensive damage to the fire-fighting equipment and this combined with a lack of water made fire-fighting impossible. In Hiroshima 70 per cent of the fire-fighting equipment was crushed in the fire-stations and 80 per cent of trained personnel were unable to respond to the fire alert. Although the pumping stations were not largely affected, serious damage was sustained by distribution pipes and mains with resulting leakage and drop in water pressure. Many of those killed immediately were either crushed or burnt to death. Of those who were burnt to death, many were trapped in buildings and would have escaped with minor injuries only had there been no fire.

Likely Effects of Thermal Radiation on Residental Buildings in the UK

Since conventional high explosive weapons emit only minute amounts of thermal radiation compared to nuclear weapons, the two small bombs dropped on Japan and nuclear weapon-testing carried out before the 1963 partial test ban treaty provide the only evidence of the likely effects of thermal radiation upon residental buildings. The effects of the larger weapons commonly held today have not been tested and can therefore only be estimated.

Not only are the weapons effects impossible to compare with weapons used in the last war; house design, materials and construction methods have also changed. Prior to 1939, houses were generally of two or three storeys, built of brick with 9 in. or 13½ in. exterior walls, 4½ in. brick interior partition walls with roofs of slates or tiles on wooden rafters. Since 1945, however, industrialised building systems together with the tendency towards high-rise development (in 1981 over 6 per cent of all UK dwellings were in blocks of flats five or more storeys high), have changed the traditional building patterns. Outer walls in modern two- and three-storey houses are now usually 8½ in. brick and block with lighter panels inserted and have a marked increase in window space responding to increasing building standard requirements for lighting and ventilation. Interior partition walls are 4 in. block and roofs are tiles on timber rafters. Lightweight houses are found in new town developments and are constructed of timber and aluminium. Modern blocks of flats have 9 in. brick or brick/block walls frequently with lightweight panels and extensive glazing. Interior partition walls are 4½ in. brick or block and upper floors rest on solid or hollow concrete floors.

However, fire was one of the major causes of death and destruction at Hiroshima and Nagasaki and it is very important to try to assess the likely effects of thermal radiation from nuclear weapons on the

UK housing stock, even though these cannot be quantified with any accuracy.

The first pulse of thermal radiation is experienced as brilliant light; this has no direct effect upon residental buildings. It may mean, however, that the occupier is temporarily blinded and is thus unable to take the necessary action to extinguish any fires started in his home. Apart from this indirect effect of the first pulse, it is the second pulse of thermal radiation, experienced as an intense wave of heat lasting several seconds, that causes much of the damage associated with nuclear weapons.

Table 2.1 gave approximate distances for the different effects of thermal radiation. The intense heat and blast experienced near ground zero will completely destroy all buildings. The effects of the heatwave are, however, more extensive than those of the blastwave and thus it is the heat effects that occur beyond the zone of irreparable blast damage that are important. The distances for such zones from the various weapon yields are set out in Table 2.1 on page 12.

The rays of heat emitted from the fireball travel in a straight line and thus only those aspects of a house in direct line with the fireball will be exposed to the heat. In Figure 2.1, for example, only the north-facing wall in House C will be exposed to the direct heat of the thermal radiation. House B will be completely protected due to the shielding effect of House C and only the upper floors of the flats in Block A would be directly exposed on their north-facing sides.

Figure 2.1: Thermal Radiation Emitted from the Fireball (not to scale)

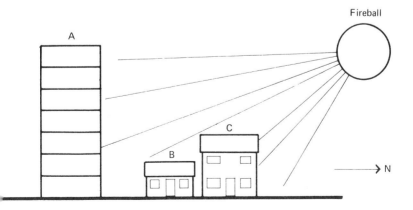

Tests carried out in the Nevada Desert in 1953 showed that wooden houses beyond the range of severe blast damage charred but did not burn;[3] even though dense black smoke was emitted, the material did not sustain ignition. It is likely therefore that the typical brick or concrete exterior of most UK houses would likewise prove resistant to thermal radiation once beyond the zone of severe blast damage. Houses that are only moderately damaged by the blastwave will still be vulnerable to exposure to thermal radiation through windows and other openings. Heat rays will pass straight through glass windows and doors and other openings and cause curtains, papers, carpets and furniture to ignite spontaneously. As stated above, houses built since 1945 have incorporated an increasingly great percentage of glazing and this presents an increased likelihood of penetration by the thermal radiation. Table 2.7 outlined the approximate distances for spontaneous ignition of paper and fabrics for different weapon yields:

up to   2.1 miles from a   20 KT weapon
up to 10.4 miles from a 500 KT weapon
up to 14.5 miles from a   1 MT weapon
up to 45.4 miles from a   10 MT weapon

Should a 1 MT weapon be exploded, houses in an area of approximately 660 square miles would be liable to extensive fire damage if no action was taken to prevent fires developing once they had started.

Once a spontaneous ignition of combustible material in a room has occurred, the material must burn vigorously for 10 to 20 minutes before room flashover occurs, i.e. when a fire confined to a single piece of furniture or part of the room suddenly spreads to fill the whole room. After room flashover, the fire becomes intense enough to penetrate interior partitions and spread to other rooms. Peak intensity of fire would be reached on average in an hour. Given that modern furniture will give off toxic fumes and proceed rapidly once the flaming stage is reached[14] (which for spontaneous ignition is, of course, immediately), the occupier will have to act extremely quickly to put out any fires caused by the heat rays. Not all houses will have windows directly facing the fireball and will therefore not experience these dangers from fire within the individual house (needless to say, no house would remain standing in any area covered by a fire-storm); however, those houses which do have windows facing the fireball are in all probability likely to have more than one, since windows tend to be concentrated in the United Kingdom on the south- and west-facing aspects of the house. It would be very difficult therefore for an occupier to cope with fires starting in two or more rooms in addition to carrying children to safety, closing doors and windows, etc. If the occupier failed to put out the fire himself, it is extremely unlikely that the fire-brigade, even if it was concerned to try to reach the house, would be able to do so. The blastwave would destroy many of the fire-stations themselves before engines could be removed, as well as making streets impassable with debris. In addition, failure of electrically-operated pumping stations and rupture of mains would cut off water supplies needed to extinguish the fires. Even simple rescues from burning buildings would be limited by the radioactive fallout within 30 minutes of the weapon exploding.

It must also be pointed out that the blastwave can start fires both inside and outside the home by overturning gas or electrical equipment, by fracturing gas mains, by causing electrical fires. The blastwave follows only seconds after the heatwave and would give very little time to even the most quick-thinking and athletic of householders to check all possible sources of fire in his home, let alone individuals who are in a state of shock and probably injured by the rapid sequence of heat- and blastwaves.

Fires started out of doors, e.g. in dried leaves or rubbish, are unlikely to cause severe damage to houses, except those caught up within a forest fire.

It has been argued that the wind associated with the blastwave will be likely to blow out the fires started by the heatwave seconds earlier. However, as the Office of Technology Assessment[4] states, studies and tests of this effect have been very contradictory, so that the extent to which blast can be relied on to extinguish fires remains quite uncertain.

Advice given by the UK government[15] to whitewash windows and remove easily combustible items from upper floors would be effective in reducing the effects of thermal radiation since the whitewash will largely reflect the heat wave. The HMSO booklet, *Nuclear Weapons*[2] claims that painting/whitewashing windows and skylights will reduce heat radiation by 80 per cent. No basis for calculation of this figure is provided and no figures to substantiate this can be found in the technical authorities on the subject.

A further effect of thermal radiation upon the UK housing stock is the creation of mass fires. As outlined earlier, the likelihood of fire-storms occurring is simply not known, although there is a very strong possibility that such fire-storms would occur in many UK cities. Fire-storms are likely to occur near to ground zero and would have the effect of reducing to ashes those houses which the blastwave had already reduced to rubble. The development of conflagrations (moving fire-fronts), however, would have the capacity to devastate areas far removed from other weapons effects.

Within the area covered by the fire-storm all buildings would be destroyed by fire, in addition, of course, to the many lives that would be lost.

Fire will also play an important part in the destruction of infrastructure necessary for water, gas and electricity provision as was outlined earlier in the section on blast damage to these services.

The Effect of Initial and Delayed Nuclear Radiation upon Residential Buildings

Radiation is perhaps the best known and most feared of the effects of nuclear weapons. Undetectable by the human senses, it can be lethal. It is, however, the effect against which effective precautions can be taken in some instances, and the vast bulk of the government's advice to the public concerning nuclear war[15] is how to protect against nuclear radiation.

Nuclear radiations are continuously emitted after the moment of detonation of a nuclear weapon; they are emitted from the fireball and eventually fall to earth. A distinction is made between that radiation which falls within the first minute after detonation (known as initial radiation) and the delayed radiation which falls to earth later and is commonly known as nuclear fallout.

Initial radiation comprises gamma rays and neutron particles. These cause severe biological damage to living cells and are lethal to humans. Since there is rapid decay of their intensity, however, they cause little harm beyond that area where other lethal bomb effects will have destroyed all living organisms. This close-range radiation is important, however, where neutron bombs are used since they are designed to enhance the prompt radiation aspects of nuclear weapons. As explained in the introduction, however, they are unlikely to be used in the United Kingdom. Initial radiation has no effect on houses or other structures and causes no physical damage.

Delayed radiation is commonly known as nuclear fallout. Fallout from a ground-burst weapon comprises molten and solidified particles of earth, thrown high into the air when the weapon exploded, onto which the radioactive products of the detonation have condensed. The particles are very small, resembling fine to coarse sand particles ranging in size from 20-700 micrometres. There are also many particles which are smaller than this, but they would remain in the stratosphere and be moved large distances by the winds there, coming down to earth months or years later with their radioactivity much reduced. Since all nuclear fallout is blown by the wind, the effects can extend many miles from the point of explosion.

In the case of an air-burst weapon where the fireball does not touch the ground, the fission products rise with the fireball into the stratosphere. They form very small particles and since there are no heavy dust particles for them to adhere to, they take many months to return to earth. There is therefore very little nuclear fallout immediately following the explosion, and when the radioactive particles do eventually return to earth, they are very widely distributed and their natural radioactivity will have declined.

Whilst the radioactive fallout represents a very severe threat to human beings, this book is concerned primarily with the effects of nuclear weapons upon people's homes. Whilst blast and heat have drastic consequences upon built structures, radioactive fallout, like the initial radiation, causes no damage whatsoever to buildings, since it is living cells that radiation has the power to destroy. All buildings therefore remain unaffected by the highly lethal radioactivity around them and it is the ability of people's homes to protect them against this radiation that is to be discussed in detail in the next chapter.

The Effect of the Electromagnetic Pulse upon Residential Housing

The OTA[4] define the electromagnetic pulse (EMP) as 'A sharp pulse of radio frequency (long wavelength) electromagnetic radiation produced when an explosion occurs in an unsymmetrical environment, especially at or near the earth's surface or at high altitudes. The intense electric and magnetic fields can damage unprotected electrical and electronic equipment over a large area.'

If a nuclear weapon is exploded at very high altitudes (i.e. above 19 miles) the EMP produced ranges hundreds or thousands of miles. Such an explosion is therefore a very likely prelude to a nuclear attack since much of the military communication will be destroyed. The exact effects are not known since only a few tests had been carried out prior to the 1963 partial test ban treaty. Modern electronic equipment is particularly susceptible to the damage it can cause; the old-fashioned thermionic valves are far less likely to be damaged. Anything with its aerial up and operating at the frequencies typical for the emergency services or the police, for example, would have its 'front end' electronics totally destroyed.

As with nuclear radiation, the EMP causes no damage to built structures whatsoever, although it may well destroy electronic equipment within them. Neither does it cause any direct harm to human beings, unlike nuclear radiation which can be lethal. The main effect on residential housing therefore is likely to be on the services supplied to the house. Anthony Tucker, in a book edited by the Royal United Services Institute,[16] notes that many vital civil systems including major refineries and the national grid are wholly dependent upon computer control which would in all probability be destroyed. In addition, if giant surges of power were transmitted through the grid (assuming that the entire network had not tripped out) consumer equipment in people's homes would be rendered useless even when power was restored. There is also little doubt that the much vaunted new electronic and computerised telephone exchanges would be put permanently out of action. Telephone links into people's homes would thus be rendered useless. Radio will also be extremely vulnerable since anything with an extended aerial and switched on will be destroyed.

Since many people will be relying on their radio, television or telephone for instructions on where to obtain food and water and generally what to do, this permanent black-out of communications is potentially as great a danger as the other effects of nuclear weapons.

References

1. Stockholm International Peace Research Institute, *Yearbook 1980, World Armaments and Disarmament* (Taylor & Francis, London, 1980).
2. Home Office and Scottish Home and Health Department, *Nuclear Weapons* (HMSO, London, 1974).
3. S. Glasstone and P.J. Dolan (eds.), *The Effects of Nuclear Weapons* (United States Department of Defense and United States Department of Energy: 3rd edition, Castle House, Tunbridge Wells, 1980).
4. Office of Technology Assessment, Congress of the United States, *The Effects of Nuclear War* (Croom Helm, London, 1980).
5. A. Tucker and J. Gleisner, *Crucible of Despair – the Effects of Nuclear War* (Menard Press, London, 1982).
6. P. Goodwin, *Nuclear War: the Facts on our Survival* (Ash & Grant, London, 1981).
7. Home Office, *Domestic Nuclear Shelters: Technical Guidance* (HMSO, London, 1981).
8. Committee for the Compilation of Materials on Damage caused by the Atomic Bombings in Hiroshima and Nagasaki, *Hiroshima and Nagasaki: The Physical,*

Medical and Social Effects of the Atomic Bombings, trans. E. Ishikawa and D.L. Swain (London, Hutchinson, 1981).

9. LATB Study Group, *London After the Bomb* (Oxford University Press, Oxford, 1982).
10. British Medical Association, *The Medical Effects of Nuclear War* (John Wiley & Sons, Chichester, 1983).
11. Home Office, *Water Services in War*, Emergency Services Circular ES6/76 (HMSO, London, 1976).
12. I. Tyrell, *The Survival Option. A Guide to Living Through Nuclear War* (Jonathan Cape, London, 1982).
13. Building Research Establishment, *Fires in Dwellings – an Investigation of Actual Fires. Part I – Hazards due to Ceiling and Roof Construction*, BRE Current Paper CP51/77 (Department of the Environment, London, 1977).
14. Building Research Establishment, *Fires in Dwellings – an Investigation of Actual Fires. Part II – Hazards from Ground-floor Fires. Part III – Physiological Effects of Fire*, BRE Current Paper CP80/78 (Department of the Environment, London, 1978).
15. Home Office, *Protect and Survive* (HMSO, London, 1980).
16. Royal United Services Institute (ed.), *Nuclear Attack: Civil Defence* (Brassey's, Oxford, 1982).

3 PROVIDING PROTECTIVE ACCOMMODATION IN THE UK IN THE EVENT OF NUCLEAR WAR

One of the primary duties of any government is to safeguard its people in time of emergency. This statutory function imposed by the 1948 Civil Defence Act is commonly referred to as civil defence or home defence. The provision of shelter for the civilian population against the effects of a nuclear explosion is only one of the many aspects of a civil defence system designed to protect people in the event of nuclear war. Other aspects include maintenance of law and order, provision of food, water and medical services for survivors, re-establishment of communications, power supplies, transport, etc.

Although this chapter is concerned primarily with those aspects of the plans for civil defence in the UK that are concerned with the provision of protective shelter both before and after a nuclear attack, a brief summary of all the major civil defence provisions in the UK is provided since it is impossible to isolate completely the effectiveness of any one single aspect of defence provision. Government plans are examined to ascertain the extent to which the government has taken any action towards providing a suitable safeguard for its civilian population and to what extent the individual must rely on his own efforts for protection.

As stated earlier, the mainstay of current government policy[1] regarding protective accommodation is that this should be provided by people's own homes; this chapter therefore will be largely concerned with the extent to which people's homes can protect them against and after a nuclear attack and what plans, if any, have been made by the government as a supplement or alternative to this policy.

Civil Defence Measures Currently Provided by the Government

Given that the responsibility for safeguarding its people in time of emergency belongs to the government, it is clearly essential to outline the civil defence preparations that this, and previous, governments have taken and which are currently in force, together with any policies or proposals which are likely to come into being during the lifetime of the current government. A succession of governments have been responsible for the current level of civil defence provision in the UK and a brief explanation is given of the post-war development of civil defence. Clearly there are many aspects of civil defence besides that of shelter provision for the population, i.e. warning and monitoring medical services, food and water supply, etc., and these will be described briefly in order that a comprehensive picture can be obtained of the full range of protective measures available to the UK population. The issue of shelter provision will be dealt with in detail.

The need for civil defence in the event of an atomic attack was widely recognised in 1945. The destruction of Hiroshima and Nagasaki was fresh in people's minds and the post-war decision to proceed with the development of a British nuclear capacity as well as the increasing number of targets on UK soil, created an awareness for the need of an effective civil defence. Campbell[2] outlines in detail the historical development of the UK civil defence system. A summary of the main stages of its development is set out in chronological order below.

The Historical Development of Civil Defence in the UK

Early 1950s
- £50 million to £100 million spent on building bunkers.
- plans for evacuation and dispersal had been prepared for people in 'priority classes'.
- a civil defence corps of over 300,000 persons was divided into five sections covering Rescue and First Aid, Ambulance and Casualty Collecting, Welfare, Warden direction for emergency services in damaged areas, HQ co-ordination of emergency services.
- emergency billeting arrangements had been made.
- food stockpiles were kept in buffer depots.
- an Auxiliary Fire Service was in existence and forward Medical Aid Units had been prepared for the NHS.

1954-9
- Development of the Backbone network was planned – i.e. a chain of new microwave radio stations which now form an extensive communications network throughout Britain (not completed until the early 1960s).
- commencement of the secret construction of 12 new underground regional seats of government, and the controlling Central Government War HQ.
- Royal Observer Corps was given the job of observing nuclear

explosions and fallout (the true nature of which had only recently been recognised) – ROC was later incorporated into the UK Warning and Monitoring Network (UKWMO).
– extensive military (as opposed to Home Office) involvement with civil defence meant that everyone in the armed forces was trained in civil defence work; 30,000 men were formed into a Mobile Defence Corps for fire-fighting, rescue and ambulance work; RAF reserve operated on emergency fire service.
– first official details on the H-bomb were made available to the public.
– sub-regional controls were introduced into the regional civil defence organisation; new vehicles were purchased for civil defence activities.

By the end of the 1950s, with the advent of missile delivery of weapons, the realisation had dawned that civil defence could do no more than provide marginal relief for the population – preservation of administration became of paramount importance, supplanting relief of survivors. Thereafter civil defence began to decline.

1960-7
– Mobile Defence Corps plus supporting units were disbanded in 1959.
– government withdrew regulations allowing local authorities to requisition shelters.
– in 1961 the Civil Defence Corps had a peak of 375,000 members – membership decreased rapidly thereafter and it was disbanded in 1968. There were 19,000 members of the Auxiliary Fire Service (also disbanded in 1968), 55,000 in the Special Constabulary + 70,000 in the NHS reserve. 4,000 units in the Industrial Civil Service have also since disappeared.
– NATO and other military exercises took place, rehearsing control of civilians in war.
– money continued to be spent on buildings and communications for emergency controls.
– government issued advice to the public on how to protect themselves in their own homes.
– UKWMO continued to be developed.
– stockpiles were run down, plans for communal shelters rejected, the evacuation and dispersal scheme was virtually abandoned.

1968
– Civil Defence was reduced to a care and maintenance basis.
– Civil Defence Corps, Auxiliary Fire Service and Home Guard

(reformed as Territorial and Army Volunteer Reserve 3) were disbanded.
- three civil defence schools and colleges closed, leaving only Easingwold.
- all government and local authority bunkers were put onto care and maintenance.
- stockpiles were maintained at a minimum level.
- UKWMO was kept going although the number of warning posts was halved.

1972-9
- Home Office (with a reorganised Emergency Services Division) set out the four objectives of home defence as:

   to take those defensive measures necessary in the UK.

   (a) to secure the UK against any internal threat;

   (b) to mitigate as far as practicable the effects of any direct attack on the UK involving the use of conventional nuclear, biological or chemical weapons;

   (c) to provide alternative machinery of government at all levels to increase the prospects of, and to direct, national survival; and

   (d) to enhance the basis for national recovery in the post-attack period (ES3/73, *Home Defence Planning Assumptions*).[3]
- average budget during these years – £15 million to £20 million p.a. This has been followed during the decade by over 60 circulars to local authorities, giving guidance as to how civil defence plans should be carried out.
- reorganisation of administrative boundaries of the sub-regions to form the present 17 sub-regions in England and Wales, three zones in Scotland and a single zone for Northern Ireland.

1979 onwards
In 1980, the newly elected Conservative government carried out a review of civil defence with the result that a Minister of State was appointed with special responsibility for civil defence; a backbench committee was to be allowed to investigate the state of civil defence and an extra £3,000,000 was made available to local authorities for planning purposes. There was increased emphasis on voluntary effort and community organisation and two new co-ordinators for voluntary effort in civil defence were appointed. In the latter part of 1980 the Home Secretary promised that the warning and monitoring organisation

would be modernised, that the public would be advised as to which shelters would be their best buys and that the government expenditure would increase from £27,000,000 p.a. to £45,000,000 p.a. (i.e. from 49p to 81p per person). New draft civil defence regulations were introduced shortly before the termination of the Conservative government term in May 1983 and reintroduced in the same form on 12 July 1983 under the newly elected Conservative administration. These draft regulations came into operation on 1 December 1983.[4,5,6,7]

Current Civil Defence Measures in the UK

There are many aspects to the provision of an adequate civil defence system for a country's population. These can be categorised as follows: (a) warning and monitoring of attack; (b) preservation of administration and systems of control; (c) welfare services for relief of survivors of attack; (d) shelter against effects of attack for civilian population. Since it is item (d) with which this report is primarily concerned, this will be dealt with in detail whereas the other three aspects will be described only briefly in order that a comprehensive picture can be given of the UK civil defence system. A much fuller examination of these aspects can be found elsewhere.[2,8,9] Appendix 2 sets out comparative details of the civil defence preparations in other European countries as well as the USA and USSR.

Warning and Monitoring Services in the UK

The UK Warning and Monitoring Organisation (UKWMO) is one of the most developed aspects of the UK civil defence system. Some 370 warning and control staff are employed by the Home Office[2] comprising 90 per cent of the Home Office staff working on civil defence. It is formed primarily from the old Royal Observer Corps whose skills in visual observation of aircraft had become obsolete in the age of high-speed jets. The tasks of the UKWMO are to observe nuclear explosions and fallout and distribute details of them to military and civil war headquarters. There are 872 warning posts throughout the UK, mostly on high land. Most of the current warning system was established in the early 1960s. A major element in this system is the Ballistic Missile Early Warning Station at Fylingdales on the east coast of Yorkshire (completed in 1964), although the earliest warning now of an impending attack is in fact more likely to come from US satellite warning systems orbiting the earth at 22,000 miles.

The amount of warning which is likely to be given has been the subject of considerable debate. Campbell[2] notes that the Scientific Advisers Training Manual issued by the Home Office Scientific Advisory Branch states that 'No particular warning time can be guaranteed, but it is expected that the warning will be given not less than *three minutes* before an attack . . .' (writer's emphasis). However, unless a nuclear weapon is released either by accident or without authorisation, it is very difficult to envisage any pre-emptive attack taking place without a considerable build up of tension or a conventional war taking place. Civil defence preparations could therefore have been in hand for at least a matter of days.

Once a hostile attack has been recognised, the warning is communicated through the network constructed in the early 1960s. Direct warning would first be passed to the UK Regional Air Operations Centre at High Wycombe and from there to 252 police stations and headquarters. From here the 7,000 warning sirens throughout the UK can be automatically set to give the air raid warning (or the all clear). These are backed up by 11,000 other warning points in rural areas. The BBC would also issue the attack warning on all its broadcasting networks.

Should any hostile attack be preceded by the explosion of a nuclear weapon at very high altitude, however, the effect of the electromagnetic pulse produced will be largely to cripple the communication system carrying the warning. Hardening of this system is now underway.

The UKWMO also collects and disseminates details of fallout and bomb bursts. Fallout warnings would be issued in any area where radioactivity rose above 0.3 Roentgens an hour.

The monitoring service is vital for those concerned with the direction of military operations in the UK as well as any attempt at survivor relief or evacuation. The three-minute warning could likewise prove of great value for military purposes. From the point of view of civilian protection, however, its only real value would be in allowing those persons out of doors to seek some form of shelter from the heat flash.

Administration and Control

In the absence of a shelter or evacuation policy for the civilian population, the emphasis in civil defence planning over recent years has been on retaining the means of regeneration. This has made it necessary to ensure the survival of some form of government as well as control of the civilian population. Campbell[2] sets out the contemporary machinery of wartime government in a diagram (Figure 3.1) showing a five-tier integrated structure of civil and military controls.

Figure 3.1: Structure of Wartime Government

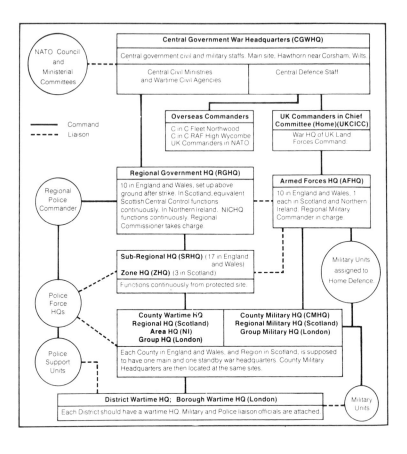

Source: D. Campbell, *War Plan U.K.*

For the purposes of administration, the country is divided into sub-regions. There are 17 sub-regions in England and Wales each with a Sub-regional Headquarters (SRHQ) (it was revealed by the 1980 Civil

Defence Exercise that three of these SRHQs had no proper head-quarters and that several others needed considerable expenditure before they could be properly used).

Scotland is divided into three zones and Northern Ireland comprises a single zone. Central Government War Headquarters are situated at Hawthorn, near Corsham, Wiltshire. However, this and other control agencies may well be primary targets of any counterforce attack and in this case the SRHQs would take over the role of government.

Home Office Circular ES7/73[10] outlines the role of SRHQs as comprising *inter alia* the administration of justice, maintenance by the police of law and order, and the general behaviour and morale of survivors. They would also be responsible for providing information on the extent and effect of the attack and determining priorities for allocation of resources.

Within the sub-region, each county would have a County Controller (the peace-time Chief Executive) who would have control over the county except for police and military matters. The general functions of both county and district levels of administration were set out in the recently published Draft Civil Defence (General Local Authority Functions) Regulations 1983 which were laid before Parliament on 12 July, 1983, and came into force on 1 December, 1983. Since these represent the most recent government policy and guidelines the major points are set out in some detail below.

County Council (including the GLC) Functions in the Event of Nuclear War

(i) To make, review and revise plans for
— Collecting information on the results of hostile attack and distributing such information.
— Controlling and co-ordinating action necessary as a result of hostile attack.
— Instructing and advising the public on the effects of hostile attack and on protective measures to be taken against such effects.
— Utilising such buildings, structures, excavations and other features of land in their area as are suitable for use for the purpose of providing civil defence shelters for the public.
— Providing and maintaining a service in their area for the rescue of persons from damaged buildings and debris in the event of hostile attack.
— Providing and maintaining a service in their area for the billeting or temporary accommodation therein and, so far as may be necessary,

the maintenance of persons who, owing to hostile attack, are made homeless.

— Providing and maintaining a service in their area for the prevention of disease, or of the spread of disease, in circumstances arising out of hostile attack, including the provision of facilities for emergency sanitation and the removal and disposal of refuse of any kind.

— Providing facilities for the disposal of human remains in the event of hostile attack.

— Providing and maintaining a service in their area for the distribution, conservation and control of food in the event of hostile attack, including emergency feeding services and equipment.

— Providing and maintaining a service in their area for the urgent repair, replacement, or demolition and clearance, as the case may be, of any property, including land, dwelling houses, or premises providing goods or services, or any street within the meaning of the Highways Act 1980(a), in circumstances arising out of hostile attack.

— Providing and maintaining any other services essential to the life of the community in the event of hostile attack.

— Securing the participation of voluntary organisations (that is to say bodies whose activities are carried on otherwise than for profit, not being public or local authorities), and other persons volunteering their services, in providing assistance to civil defence services formed in the event of hostile attack or a threat of hostile attack.

(ii) To establish, equip, and maintain in premises in two places in the county (five places in Greater London) an emergency centre in which to control and co-ordinate action to be taken by them in the event or threat of hostile attack.

(iii) To arrange for training of an appropriate number of suitable members of their own staff plus the staff of every district in the county (London Borough of the GLC) for purposes of carrying out plans in (i) above.

(iv) To send on the appropriate training courses staff who, by the nature of their wartime responsibilities, have been designated as needing government training.

(v) To take part in any civil defence training exercises.

(vi) To make arrangements for volunteers to be trained.

District Council (including London Boroughs and the City of London) Functions in the Event of Nuclear War

(i) to supply any information requested by their County Council.

(ii) to assist at the request of the Minister or County Council in making plans listed in (i) above and carrying out of volunteer training.

(iii) carrying out of plans prepared by the County Council.

(iv) Establish, equip and maintain an emergency centre in their area in which to control and co-ordinate action to be taken by them in the event or threat of hostile attack.

(v) Arrange for training of a suitable number of staff as well as all staff who, by the nature of their wartime responsibilities, have been designated as needing government training.

(vi) To take part in any training exercises.

The funds provided to carry out such tasks were set out in the Draft Civil Defence (Grant) (Amendment) Regulations 1983 which likewise came into operation on 1 December, 1983.

Complete reimbursement of all costs incurred by local and police authorities in the discharge of their civil defence functions is given for: provision of communications equipment for civil defence purposes; provision of training for local authority staff, police forces and special constables and participation in training exercises (excluding salary payments); attendance of members of staff at training courses; reimbursement of volunteers' expenses. All other expenses incurred by way of carrying out civil defence functions are given 75 per cent grants.

In effect it would seem therefore that the present county councils are responsible for the preparation of plans and it is the task of the district councils actually to carry out the plans as far as possible in their area.

Responsibility for law and order comes under military control: all organisations involved would be expected to work together in the event of war. Guidelines as to what sort of plans should be produced are given in government circulars. A list of all such circulars is provided in Appendix 3; further details are not given here.

Whilst these guidelines would seem to provide a thoroughly planned and prepared civil defence programme, a variety of factors, including lack of money and lack of political motivation, have prevented any noticeable increase in the protection available to the UK citizen. There is widespread lack of confidence in Home Office advice: this was acknowledged in the parliamentary debate on civil defence held on 24 March, 1983,[2] where it was stated by Mr Neil Thorne (Chairman of the Council for Civil Defence) that a new document giving advice to the public should, it was hoped, be available before the end of the year (unavailable as at 1 September, 1983). More than 100 local authorities of all political complexions have refused to co-operate with government plans, predominantly on the grounds that given the level of funding available no adequate protection can be provided and it would be wrong to encourage the population into thinking it had. Some district councils have made their war plans publicly available as a means of showing their inadequacy. The lack of effective co-ordination between the large number of government departments involved at both national and local level has been widely criticised.

There is also a lack of organisation at district and metropolitan borough level. While counties have Emergency Planning Officers who spend at least some of their time on civil defence, the situation at district level is far less satisfactory, since virtually nothing appears to be happening. Most districts have selected a wartime headquarters – many of these, however, are above ground and have no communications equipment installed. A booklet produced by the Conservative Political Centre[1] states that most local authorities have no plans on how to administer their area, no surveys of possible shelters have been undertaken, few authorities appear to know what food or fuel stores exist in their areas, whether any local communications equipment exists, etc.

Since all local authorities are being pressured to reduce expenditure in line with the current government's policy of restraint on public expenditure, making finance available for such relatively unlikely events as nuclear war comes low on a list of priorities which include housing, education, transport, public health, etc. This lack of resources is illustrated by the results of a survey carried out to investigate how local authorities had responded to the government circular ES3/81 – *Protection of the General Public in War*.[13] This circular asked local authorities to carry out a survey of the protective qualities of the residential accommodation in their area in order to identify the available protection for the population. Guidance was provided in the form of a booklet entitled *Protective Qualities of Buildings*,[14] which identified 18 basic types of building and their associated protective values. In all, 10 per cent of all district councils were contacted to ascertain the results of this survey. Replies were received from over 50 per cent of the authorities, only two of whom had even started the survey, let alone completed it (one of the two councils actually to have started noted that it had 37,000 domestic properties in its area and that it would therefore be a very long while before the survey was completed). The reasons given for not having undertaken the survey were in all cases lack of resources – of both money and time.

Given the level of funding available it has proved impossible for local authorities to carry out all of the functions required of them by central government. Indeed, very few local authorities have any thorough or effective civil defence preparations at all. This is not surprising since it was realised back in the 1960s that adequate protection of the population was virtually impossible in the event of nuclear war and emphasis was switched from survivor relief to the maintenance of administration and control. Preparations have therefore been made by central government in order to protect those persons who would be responsible for post-attack regeneration of the UK. These preparations are outlined in detail by Laurie[9] and Campbell[2] and only a brief summary is set out below.

The Protection of Government in the Event of Nuclear War

Preparations to ensure the preservation of civil and military control have been underway since the 1950s. The wartime national seat of government (Central Government War Headquarters – CGWHQ) is at Hawthorn, near Corsham (90 miles west of London). Since this is likely to be a prime target in the event of a hostile attack, an attempt has been made to disperse as many separate government and command centres as possible. These are predominantly to the west of London and include Air Defence HQ at Bentley Priory, Strike Command at High Wycombe, UK Land Forces HQ at Wilton and the General Communications HQ at Cheltenham, as well as the protected sites at Harwell and Aldermaston Research Stations. In addition to these national command centres there are the regional and sub-regional headquarters. The sub-regional HQs (SRHQs) are the main centres for civilian control and relief in the UK and are the focus for whatever civil defence services will be available. A sub-regional commissioner (a senior civil servant) will be in charge and will have complete autonomy over civilian matters until links with a higher level of government can be established. There are at present 21 of these SRHQs with a further one still to be built. Only four of these 21 have been purpose built, the others are largely converted from RAF facilities or Second World War cold stores. The purpose-built ones are located in two-storey concrete basements below government office blocks with walls 20-30 inches thick. Each has its own borehole for water. Some 150,000 gallons of water are stored permanently and a generator room provides the necessary power. Air conditioning and filtering facilities are incorporated. A radio mast and small broadcasting studio provide the necessary communications. No food supplies are stored in the bunkers, however. These bunkers are for the protection of designated staff (selected not on a personal basis but rather because they hold a particular post) but not for their families. At each of the bunkers, an Assistant Chief Constable would be in charge of a small police team who would remain independent of the sub-regional commissioner. At regional level there are bunkers for military personnel only.

Extensive plans have been made both for the provision of hardened bunkers and communications systems for the key personnel of central government within London and for the evacuation of such personnel, should there be sufficient warning, to the protected command centres to the north and west of London. Central Government War HQ at Hawthorn is a huge complex situated underground, beneath old stone quarries, which is capable of housing 20,000 government staff. Purified water supplies and sophisticated air filtration would ensure months of protection providing there was not a successful direct attack upon the site. All aspects of the war and recovery would be directed from this Central War HQ in conjunction with the NATO allies. Defence staff and military commanders, Foreign Office officials (international relations) and Department of Trade officials (shipping and trade to and from the UK) would be based here as well as representatives of the Home Office, Environment and Energy Departments. Considerable publicity has surrounded the bunker recently completed at High Wycombe, the UK Strike Command HQ for NATO.

The maintenance of law and order will be of great importance in the period following an attack and it will be the joint responsibility of the military and the police. These are commanded from the regional rather than the sub-regional level. Campbell[2] notes that the Police Manual of Home Defence outlines the major tasks of the police force in the event of nuclear war as:

(a) special measures to maintain internal security, with particular reference to the detention or restriction of movement of subversive or potentially subversive people;
(b) the guarding of key points and the maintenance of protected areas;
(c) manning carrier control and carrier receiver points;
(d) supplementing public warnings;
(e) the control of essential service routes;
(f) assisting the armed forces in their mobilisation plans;
(g) advice to the public;
(h) collection and distribution of radiac instruments and maroons;
(i) freezing of petrol filling stations.

The essential service routes are a co-ordinated network of major roads which would be kept clear for essential traffic between ports, airports, depots, bases, etc. Control of these roads would effectively limit any large-scale attempt at self-evacuation.

The police and military will have a monopoly on coercive power which would be used to control movement of supplies and protection of the means of administration and control against any desperate measures likely to be used by the survivors. The government anticipates that any volunteers currently being trained would be able to assist in the more minor aspects of control and supervision should the need arise.

Welfare Services for Relief of Survivors

It has long been accepted government thinking that only very limited relief can be made available to any survivors. Individuals are told how to provide their own protection against a nuclear attack[15,16] and given lists of requirements needed for the first 14 days after the attack. No mention is made of what happens after the period of self-reliance is past.

It is the task of local government to provide whatever services it can after a hostile attack. Central government has issued a series of circulars giving instructions as to what services would be needed and how they should be provided. It has, however, made only very limited finance available to carry out these instructions and very little preparation has in fact been made by local authorities to provide any effective relief.

The provision of supplies of food and water would be of utmost importance in ensuring the survival of civilians. The Home Office Circular *Water Services in War*[17] notes that the normal distribution of water will almost certainly be destroyed in the target areas and surroundings. Once the piped water distribution system has collapsed, the fire service is responsible for distributing any available water. Supplies of available water will have been in many cases contaminated by fallout or polluted with the collapse of the sewage-disposal system; in practice, distribution will be extremely difficult because of street blockages and the very small number of vehicles likely to be available after the attack for carrying water. Since the body's reserves of water are used up within 7-10 days, those who have been unable to make provision for their own supply for the first 14 days after an attack will probably not survive.

There will also be major shortages of food in both the short and long term and many people will go hungry. It is a matter of weeks, however, before lack of food will cause death under normal conditions, although there will be a rapid decline in stamina and morale. This will be even more marked in those survivors of any nuclear attack. Emergency stockpiles of food are maintained by the government and would be greatly enlarged during any period of heightened tension likely to lead to war. Stocks of food would be earmarked and requisitioned. It is during this period of tension that the public would be expected to provide their own personal 14 days' supply; the government states in its circular on *Food and Agriculture Controls in War*[18] that 'food would be scarce and no arrangements could ensure that every surviving household would have, say, fourteen days supply of food after an attack'.

Following an attack, once the radioactivity levels had declined sufficiently, emergency feeding arrangements would begin. The school meals services are generally charged with providing the emergency feeding service. There is no explanation, however, as to where the food will be coming from or what happens when government stockpiles run low. The major stocks now kept in the MAFF buffer depots are flour, margarine and fats, sugar, sweet biscuits and a little yeast. Many of these depots, however, are of relatively flimsy construction and could well be destroyed by even minor overpressure levels. Very little government attention seems to have been given to the long-term problems involved in re-establishing the food production and processing system. It would clearly have to be a far cry from the present agricultural system based upon the petroleum and chemical industries.

These problems are set out in detail by Dr A. Jackson[19] in his study of feeding the UK after a nuclear attack: he concludes that the UK government has a far from 'credible home defence posture'.

One of the main welfare services which would be required subsequent to a nuclear attack of any scale would be skilled medical services; hospitals, equipment (especially that to deal with burns), drugs and skilled personnel would all be needed. A recent report produced by the British Medical Association's Board of Science and Education, *The Medical Effects of Nuclear War*,[20] covered in great detail and with great thoroughness and practicality the problems that would face the National Health Service subsequent to a nuclear attack. In conclusion the report states:

> The NHS could not deal with the casualties that might be expected following the detonation of a single one megaton weapon over the U.K. It follows that multiple nuclear explosions over several, possibly many, cities would force a breakdown in medical services across the

country as a whole.

There is no possibility of increasing the production of certain drugs in a short period of tension before a war, and if we wish to have large quantities of blood products available for transfusion purposes or the bulk of the present generation of medical practitioners in the country trained for certain eventualities, then all of these things would have to be done now and the country must exist on a more or less permanent emergency footing.

We believe that such a weight of nuclear attack would cause the medical services in the country to collapse. The provision of individual medical or nursing attention for victims of a nuclear attack would become remote. At some point it would disappear completely and only the most primitive first aid services might be available from a fellow survivor.

Another service essential to any survivors would be the restoration of a healthy environment. Widespread damage to the public water supply and sewage-disposal systems will create serious environmental health problems, which will be exacerbated by the large numbers of unburied corpses. Urgent measures will be needed to prevent the spread of disease among a malnourished population. Arrangements would need to be made for the collection and disposal of human waste. The government circular on *Environmental Health in War*[21] sets out the problems and is realistic in assessing the dangers likely to occur: 'enteric infections . . . coupled with the lack of proper sanitary facilities, could spread rapidly to assume epidemic proportions'. Cholera, typhoid, hepatitis, dysentry and respiratory problems are all likely to occur. The fact that rats and insects are more resistant to radiation than human beings only increases the likelihood of widespread disease. Exactly how a sanitary environment is restored in view of a lack of the necessary personnel, equipment and supplies is not explained and like most of the other life-supporting services seems to have been left to the ingenuity of those who happen to be in charge at the time.

Shelter Against the Effects of Attack, for the Civilian Population

As was explained in previous sections, government civil defence measures are aimed at providing only the essential leadership and command personnel with specific protection against the effects of nuclear attack. Warning of any impending attack will be given to as many of the civilian population as possible who are then expected to follow government instructions to stay in their homes, preferably in the innermost part of the refuge room that they had constructed in the prior days or weeks. Government advice to the public[15] stresses that individuals must remain in their homes rather than attempt to flee to other areas where they perceive the dangers to be less. People's homes are the only form of protection for the vast majority of the population and this section will therefore consider exactly what protection is available to the population.

An individual may decide however that he wishes to purchase or make a blast-proof shelter for the protection of himself and his family. The protection afforded by such shelters is dealt with in detail in the next chapter; this section is concerned solely with that form of protection upon which the vast proportion will be forced to rely – their own homes.

Chapter 2 outlined in detail the four major effects of nuclear weapons that are capable of causing widescale death and destruction. These are blast, heat, radiation and the electromagnetic pulse. Only the first three of these can directly kill human beings and therefore this chapter will consider in turn the protection afforded to a family, by their home, against: (a) the heatwave from the nuclear explosion; (b) the blastwave from the nuclear explosion; (c) the radioactive fallout which may occur up to several hours after the explosion itself and occur many miles from the point of explosion itself.

Virtually all of the advice made available to the public is concerned with this third aspect – protection against radioactive fallout. Protective factors have even been calculated on a quasi-mathematical basis for different types of dwellings and published primarily for local authority guidance.[14] Very little advice is given on how to protect oneself effectively against the effects of heat and blast. This chapter examines critically the effectiveness of a house in providing protection against all three weapons effects.

In all three cases the protection provided will vary according to the type of house. Design, age, construction materials and methods will all affect its ability to provide suitable protection. However, these detailed variations will be dealt with separately under the three separate headings.

Protection Against the Thermal Radiation Effects of Nuclear Weapons

The effects of thermal radiation from a nuclear weapon are the first to be experienced and occur within seconds of its explosion. Protection is needed first, against the brilliant flash of light which can cause temporary blindness; secondly, against the direct effects of heat upon the body; and thirdly, against the general destructive effects of fire.

This section is concerned to identify the extent to which people's homes provide them with the necessary protection against these three major effects of thermal radiation.

Protection Against Light Flash

As explained in Chapter 2, the first pulse of thermal radiation is experienced as brilliant light which can cause temporary blindness. Damage is only caused, however, if a person is looking directly at the source of light. Any person who is inside his house, unless he is looking through a window or open door, will be protected against the effects of the flash of light. Anyone who is following government instructions and is sheltering within an inner refuge room will most certainly be protected against this flash of light.

Protection against the Direct Effects of the Heat Flash

The direct effects of heat flash are taken here to mean the effects of the heat flash directly on the body, as opposed to the effects of heat caused by burning buildings, etc., which is dealt with below. Thermal radiation is emitted in straight lines from the fireball and unless reflected will burn only those things in a direct line from the fireball. Many of the casualties at Hiroshima and Nagasaki were caused by direct burns on the bodies of those out of doors at the moment of explosion. Two-thirds of the fatalities on the first day at Hiroshima were due to burns. Burns can be classified into three types – first degree burns are equivalent to bad sunburn and whilst painful do no permanent damage. Second degree burns involve partial thickness skin loss with pain and blistering, with burns over 15-20 per cent of the body surface: the main risk to life is fluid loss in the first 48 hours; infection is common and can be fatal. Third degree burns involve whole thickness skin loss. There is less pain but fluid loss and infection always occur, scarring is certain. Without specialised nursing and antibiotics to cope with the infections death would be virtually certain.

Table 2.1 on page 12 showed the extent to which first degree burns (skin reddening) and third degree burns (skin charring) occur for different size weapons. It can be seen that even for a 1 MT weapon, third degree burns (and thus very likely death) will occur up to 8 miles from ground zero, i.e. anyone outside with exposed skin in an area covering over 200 square miles would be likely to die. As important as the total amount of heat received, however, is the area of the body on which it falls, damage to the hands, face and joints being the most difficult to overcome. It is of course the hands and face that are most commonly uncovered when out of doors. Obviously time of day and year will greatly affect the number of casualties; no damage however will be caused by this direct heat flash to all those people who are shielded from it, by a building, hill, tree, etc. Greater protection is provided for those sheltering within a building, since being totally enclosed (unless the occupant is in line with an open door or window) also protects against reflected thermal radiation.

Clearly government advice to seek protection within an inner refuge room would provide total protection against these direct effects of heat flash.

In both this case and that of the flash of light described above, the vital aspect in providing protection for the population is to ensure that adequate warning is provided (and heeded) for people to seek the safety of their homes or other suitable buildings.

Protection Against the General Effects of Fire

Whilst people's homes are shown to provide effective protection in the case of heat and light flash, they obviously provide no further protection against anything once they have caught fire themselves.

The likelihood of buildings catching fire and of the development of mass fires was described in Chapter 2, and whilst this cannot be ascertained with accuracy, it was noted that houses in an area of approximately 660 square miles around a 1 MT explosion would be liable to extensive fire damage and that the development of mass fires over a smaller area around ground zero is a strong possibility. A house within the area covered by a fire-storm offers no protection at all, since all buildings within the area of the fire-storm will be consumed by fire. Likewise a house in the path of a moving fire-front provides no protection for its occupants.

In an area where only some houses have been set alight by the thermal radiation, the non-burning houses will provide protection for their occupants. Whether or not these houses catch fire themselves depends to a large extent on factors such as proximity to burning houses, windspeed and direction, design and construction materials of the non-burning houses and the occupant's ability to extinguish small fires in and around his home. Government advice to whitewash windows and remove inflammable items from upper storeys will reduce the risk of fire, but this would only really have any noticeable impact at several miles from ground zero. Nearer than this only the most resistant of houses will be able to withstand the intense heat.

Two-thirds of the 76,000 buildings in Hiroshima were destroyed by fire and 25 per cent of Nagasaki's 51,000 buildings were also totally destroyed with many seriously damaged. Many of the population who died did so because they were burned to death in collapsed buildings where they were trapped.

People's homes therefore can be seen to offer limited protection only against the effects of thermal radiation with no protection at all for those houses near the ground zero which are likely to be caught up in some form of mass fire.

Protection Against the Blast Effects of Nuclear Weapons

The blastwave from the nuclear weapon arrives seconds after the heatwave has passed. Chapter 2 outlined in detail the effects that the blastwave will have upon the typical housing stock in the UK.

In the case of a 1 MT air-burst explosion, houses will be totally destroyed for 2.65 miles from ground zero (i.e. over an area of 22 square miles), they will be irreparably damaged for 3.75 miles (i.e. over a further area of 22 square miles). Moderate to severe damage will occur up to 9.1 miles from ground zero (i.e. over a further area of 216 square miles) and light damage will extend for 15 miles from ground zero (i.e. over a further area of 446 square miles), giving a total area of damage of 706 square miles.

Government advice to the public is to stay hidden in their own homes in the refuge room constructed under the stairs or under tables/ doors reinforced by heavy objects. In the areas of light or moderate blastwave damage, typical damage will include doors and windows being blown out, tiles torn off the roof and cracked masonry. By sheltering in the refuge room, injuries caused by flying glass and masonry will be largely avoided. These could likewise be avoided by sheltering in a basement (where available) or in the understairs cupboard without any reinforcement. The key to protection is again shown to be that adequate warning must be given and heeded. In the zones of total destruction houses would be reduced entirely to rubble and would offer very little further protection. It has been noted, however,[9] that during heavy bombing in the Second World War the staircase was strong enough to support the debris that fell on it so that relatively few fatalities occurred directly as a result of house collapse, due to the efficient operation of digging-out teams. Since the weight of houses has, if anything, been reduced since 1945 and the weight in any case is not affected by the size of weapon that demolishes the house, it could be said that the refuge room under the stairs would also provide suitable protection against the blast effects of nuclear weapons. This, however, does not take account of the two other effects of nuclear weapons – thermal radiation and radioactive fallout – neither of which were associated with the conventional bombs used in the Second World War. The fact that extensive fires are burning and that lethal fallout is occurring greatly reduces the possibility that anyone at all will be dug out of their collapsed homes; given their exposed position, many of those trapped in their homes will either suffer lethal exposure to radiation or severe burns, both of which would quickly prove fatal in the absence of medical services. This in fact was the experience at Hiroshima where the actual collapse of buildings due to the blastwave was not responsible directly for the fatalities but rather that the trapped and injured were burned alive; even those able to free themselves suffered severe radiation exposure and consequent death.

There is no way that the householder can appreciably increase his house's resistance to the force of the blastwave of the nuclear attack. There is no shielding effect which would protect his house as with the heatwave; the increased air pressure (static overpressure) will apply equally on all buildings and the high-speed winds (dynamic over-pressure) would surround individual buildings virtually equally. The only options available to the householder (assuming he has sufficient notice of a hostile attack) are self-evacuation to an area he perceives as being less likely to suffer or the construction of some form of blast-proof shelter. This possibility is discussed in detail in Chapter 4.

Very little guidance has been provided by the government as to exactly what protection people's homes offer against the blastwave; this is in all probability due to the fact that people's homes in fact offer very little protection indeed against the effects of blast as compared to that provided by blast-proof shelters. Very little can be done to increase the extent of the protection currently afforded. The government, although continually pressed to provide specifically designed blast-proof accommodation, argues that it is prevented from doing this on the grounds of cost. It is officially estimated[22] that the full cost of providing shelters across Britain against nuclear attack either on a communal basis or for individual families living remotely and unpro-tected would be between £60,000m and £80,000m, i.e. £1,000-£1,500 per head of population (1980 prices). At present total expenditure on civil defence is less than £1 per head.

Protection Afforded by People's Homes Against Direct Radiation and Radioactive Fallout

The Effects of Radiation

As outlined in Chapter 2, the radiation emitted from the explosion of a nuclear weapon comprises two distinct types. First, the initial radiation which is extremely intense but limited in range, and secondly, the delayed radiation or radioactive fallout which comprises molten and solidified particles of earth, thrown high into the air when the weapon exploded, onto which the radioactive products of the detonation have condensed. The destructive power of these products decays with time, however, and the danger is therefore progressively reduced.

Whilst radiation does not affect non-living matter and therefore has no effect on houses themselves, it can be lethal for living beings. Its effect is to damage or destroy the internal structure of cells: blood cell production in particular is impaired and the stomach and intestine linings degenerate. Bacteria, however, are largely resistant to radiation and therefore in conjunction with the fact that the body's defence mechanisms are greatly reduced, the danger of infection is very serious indeed. The effects of radiation vary according to the dosage received, although the very young and old, the injured and the sick are more likely to die at a given dose rate. The medical effects at different dose rates are set out in Table 3.1.

The dose rate at any particular time will depend on the type of radioactive particles present and the extent to which they have decayed. For a 1 MT explosion at one hour after the burst the Home Office calculates[23] that:

an area of   20 sq. miles would experience 3,000 r per hour
an area of   90 sq. miles would experience 1,000 r per hour
an area of   300 sq. miles would experience   300 r per hour
an area of   900 sq. miles would experience   100 r per hour
an area of 2,000 sq. miles would experience   30 r per hour
an area of 4,500 sq. miles would experience   10 r per hour

This rate would decline with time as the radioactive elements decay; it is, however, cumulative, although a dose protracted over a longer period will tend to be less damaging than a similar single dose. The assumption that has been made by the Home Office until recently to calculate casualties is that an exposure to a total of 450 rads over two weeks will kill 50 per cent of a healthy, fit population and that exposure to 600 rads and over will kill virtually 100 per cent. Recent evidence, as discussed in the BMA Report,[20] indicates that these may well be under-estimates. It is assumed, however, that after two weeks the damage which can be done by the radioactive fallout has declined to such a level as not to represent a significant danger to human beings. It is Home Office policy to give the 'all-clear' message in a locality when the dose rate is ½ rad per hour. In a study carried out of the effects of an attack on London, however, it was shown (see Figure 3.2) that for many areas this 'safe' dose would not be achieved until much longer than 14 days after the attack.

Table 3.1: Medical Effects of Radiation

Dose (rads)	Symptoms	Deaths (average)
0-100	Men become temporarily sterile in 20-50 rads range	0
100-200	Nausea and vomiting within 3-6 hours of receiving dose and lasting less than 1 day, followed by no symptoms for 2 weeks. Recurrence of symptoms for another 4 weeks. Number of white blood cells reduced.	0
200-600	Nausea and vomiting lasting 1-2 days. No symptoms for 1-4 weeks followed by a recurrence of symptoms for up to 8 weeks. Diarrhoea, severe reduction of white blood cells, blood blisters on skin, bleeding, infection. Loss of hair above 300 rads.	0-98% in 2-12 weeks from internal bleeding or infection
600-1,000	Nausea and vomiting starting within ½ hr of receiving dose of radiation and lasting 2 days. No symptoms for 5-10 days then same symptoms as for 200-600 rads for 1-4 weeks	98-100% from internal bleeding or infection
1,000-5,000	Nausea and vomiting starting within ½ hour of receiving dose and lasting less than a day. No symptoms for about 7 days then diarrhoea, fever, disturbed salt balance in blood for 2-14 days.	100% within 14 days from collapse of circulation
more than 5,000	Nausea and vomiting immediately followed by convulsions, loss of control of movement and lethargy.	100% in 48 hours from failure of breathing or brain damage

Source: *London After the Bomb.*

Figure 3.2: When is it Safe to Come Out?

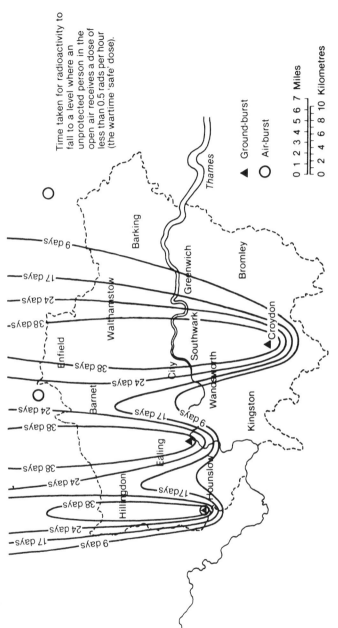

Time taken for radioactivity to fall to a level where an unprotected person in the open air receives a dose of less than 0.5 rads per hour (the wartime 'safe' dose).

▲ Ground-burst
○ Air-burst

0 1 2 3 4 5 6 7 Miles
0 2 4 6 8 10 Kilometres

Source: *London After the Bomb*, Fig. 14, p. 54.

Further detailed information on the radiation effects can be found in many sources including *Nuclear Radiation in Warfare*.[24]

How to Protect Against the Effects of Radiation

Protection against the effects of the initial nuclear radiation is academic in that, since its effects decay very rapidly, anyone near enough to ground zero to experience this radiation will be certainly killed by other effects of the nuclear weapon in any case.

It is however possible to protect oneself against the effects of radioactive fallout. It is in fact advice for protection against this radioactive fallout that is contained in the government leaflet *Protect and Survive*[15] — in the 30-page booklet only one page is concerned with blast and heat, the remainder deals with fallout.

Unlike the effects of heat and blast, the damage done by the fallout from a nuclear weapon extends many miles from the point of explosion, since the dangerous radioactive fallout can be blown many miles by the wind. Idealised and actual dose rate contours are shown in Figure 3.3.

Figure 3.3: Idealised and Actual Dose Rate Contours for a 10 MT 50% Fission Ground-burst Weapon (windspeed 30 m.p.h.)

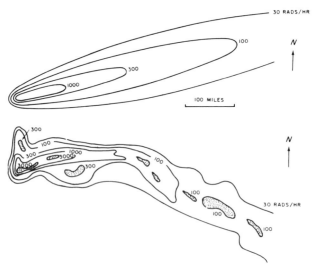

Source: Glasstone and Dolan, *The Effects of Nuclear Weapons*, Fig. 9.100a and 100b, p. 434.

Figures 3.2 and 3.3 show that in reality local weather conditions and local variations in relief cause a much more complex pattern than that of the idealised cigar-shaped patterns. It must be remembered, however, that extensive fallout is not an inevitable accompaniment to a nuclear attack. If the weapon is air burst, dust is sucked up into the atmosphere and therefore the radioactive particles have no heavy dust on which to descend rapidly to earth and will drift in the stratosphere for months, thereby losing much of their harmful potential.

It is however equally possible to have bombs which are designed to produce large amounts of fallout (the 'dirty' fission-fusion-fission bombs) or large amounts of initial radiation (the neutron bomb), both of which cause vast casualties from their radioactivity.

The most effective protection against radiation is not to receive it, i.e. for the radiation to be absorbed before it reaches the body. This is done by being as far as possible from the fallout and having a dense thickness of material between the body and the fallout, since the radioactivity is progressively reduced as it passes through this material. The denser and heavier the material, the less is required to reduce the intensity by a given amount. Table 3.2 shows the thickness required of different materials to reduce the radiation intensity by 50 per cent.

Table 3.2: Relative Protective Values — Thickness Required to Reduce Radiation Intensity by 50%

Material	Inches of Material Required
Lead	0.5
Steel	0.7
Tiles	1.0 – 1.9
Asbestos sheet	2.0
Asphalt	2.2
Concrete	2.2
Stone	2.2
Brickwork	2.8
Sand	2.9
Earth	3.3
Plaster	3.5
Slates	3.5
Wood	8.8

Source: Home Office, *Domestic Nuclear Shelters*.

One of the major problems in avoiding radiation is that it is not perceptible to the senses; it cannot be seen, smelt, tasted or touched and can only be identified and measured using specialised equipment. A large British telecommunications firm has recently started manufacturing dose rate meters to measure radiation doses — (the PDRM82) at a cost of £120 per unit (portable device) or £170 (fixed unit with remote detector and cable assembly for use in shelters) (March 1983 prices). Manufacture is being carried out for the Home Office as well as the general public and a total of 80,000 instruments are being produced in the next two to three years.

Fallout *can* sometimes be seen in the form of dust, which tends to be deposited on flat or gently sloping surfaces and will eventually be washed into drains and sewers by the rain, where it will continue to decay until it is harmless.

The Protection Afforded by People's Homes Against Radioactive Fallout

The protection afforded by a building against gamma radiation can be expressed as the 'protective factor' (PF) of that building. This is the factor by which the dose rate received by a person in the building is reduced as compared to that received by a person standing outside. A protective factor of 20 therefore means that if the outside radiation is at a rate of 400 rads/hour (which would cause death within hours) the corresponding rate indoors (in the refuge room) would be only 20 rads/hour, which given the rate of decay (by a factor of 10 as the time lengthens by a factor of 7 — for example, assuming an initial dose rate of 400 rads/hour; seven hours after the burst this will have reduced to 40 rads/hour, after 49 hours (approx. 2 days) it will be 4 rads/hour and after 343 hours (approx. 14 days) it will be 0.4 rads/hour), would not give enough accumulated radiation to cause death. However, it may well lead to the development of cancers in later years, as has been shown by the Hiroshima and Nagasaki experience.

The Home Office have produced a series of protective values for different types of dwelling. The method used for doing this is a complicated calculation involving size, type, weight and thickness of construction materials, full details of which are given in Chapter 9 of *Nuclear Weapons*.[26] The Home Office Scientific Advisory Branch have produced an illustrated document giving guidance as to the protective qualities of 18 basic housing types typically found in the United Kingdom.[14] The protective factors as calculated on the government's formula are set out in Table 3.3.

Table 3.3: Dwelling Types and their Protective Factors

Dwelling type	Protective Factor (upper figure — suburb) (lower figure — central)							
	Basement		Ground floor		First floor		Second floor	
	NA	WB	NA	WB	NA	WB	NA	WB
Caravan	—	—	1.4	1.4	—	—	—	—
	—	—	1.8	1.9	—	—	—	—
1 storey lightweight	—	—	1.9	1.9	—	—	—	—
	—	—	2.5	2.6	—	—	—	—
1 storey modern	—	—	5	6	—	—	—	—
	—	—	6	7	—	—	—	—
1 storey traditional	—	—	8	11	—	—	—	—
	—	—	9	13	—	—	—	—
2 storey lightweight	—	—	2.3	2.3	3	3	—	—
	—	—	3	3	3	3	—	—
2 storey modern detached	—	—	5	7	6	6	—	—
	—	—	6	10	7	7	—	—
2 storey modern other	—	—	8	11	6	7	—	—
	—	—	9	13	9	9	—	—
2 storey traditional detached	90	120	9	19	9	10	—	—
	90	120	12	24	11	12	—	—
2 storey traditional other	90	120	17	25	14	15	—	—
	90	120	21	30	16	16	—	—
2 storey concrete floors	180	220	26	26	24	24	—	—
	180	220	34	34	26	26	—	—
3 storey lightweight	—	—	2.3	2.4	3	3	2.9	2.9
	—	—	3	3	4	4	4	4
3 storey modern	—	—	18	19	10	11	5	5
	—	—	22	23	19	19	7	7
3 storey traditional detached	120	160	12	26	14	15	9	10
	120	160	15	33	17	18	10	11
3 storey traditional other	120	160	18	33	18	20	12	12
	120	160	22	40	23	23	14	14
3 storey concrete floors	240	300	35	35	73	73	36	36
	240	300	45	45	100	100	43	43
	Basement		Ground		Middle		Top	
4+ storey traditional	150	270	16	36	18	21	12	12
	150	270	22	51	24	24	14	14
4+ storey concrete floors	600	800	44	63	290	300	34	34
	600	800	82	110	430	430	87	87
3-4 storey stone-built (Scotland)	170	270	17	110	20	24	12	12
	150	270	22	130	26	27	14	14

NA = No action taken in blocking windows
WB = Windows blocked in the shelter room
Source: HMSO, *The Protective Qualities of Buildings*.

Clearly the safest place to be is in the basement; very few houses however have basements – the *Greater London Housing Condition Survey* of 1981[27] shows that only 3½ per cent of London houses have a basement suitable for simple shelters.

These figures produced by the government, however, relate to buildings where special modifications have been made to enable them to serve as fallout shelters. It is assumed that windows and external doorways have been blocked and that a 'refuge room' has been built in the best possible place in the building. Instructions as to how to build this refuge room are given in the *Protect and Survive* leaflet.[15] The refuge room would be lined with dense materials – heavy furniture, books, bags of earth or sand, etc.

The government assumes, moreover, that in calculating these protective factors no fallout enters the building or is deposited on walls, window sills or other projections. This is clearly an incorrect assumption since roof tiles will be shed and windows broken in zones of the lightest damage (i.e. reaching up to 15 miles from the point of explosion of a 1 MT air burst and thus covering an area of 706 square miles).

The assumption that all households will be able, or want, to construct a suitable refuge room given sufficient time (which of course may well be not available) is also open to question. The elderly and infirm would be incapable of moving heavy furniture or sandbags. Many others would simply not heed government advice, preferring to try to flee to safer areas or to seek relatives, knowing that attempts at protection were virtually impossible or believing that rapid death was in any case the most desirable option in the event of all-out nuclear war.

A further assumption made by the government is that people stay inside the shelter for the entire danger period. The protective factor is clearly only applicable as long as people stay inside the shelter. Whilst radiation sickness is not contagious, those people who go outside and return into the shelter bring contaminated particles on their body and clothes, thus reducing the PF and the safety of others in the shelter.

Life in the shelter will be extremely cramped and unpleasant, and survivors are likely to suffer extreme psychological stress caused by concern over missing family or friends, lack of outside information and general illness. Sickness and diarrhoea could be brought on by shock, by infection (due to reduced capacity to fight it) or due to a fatal radiation dose. Parents would have to watch their children suffer and die, since the young are more susceptible to the damaging effects of radiation. Brief visits outside to dispose of waste matter or dead bodies would therefore provide the only relief from the claustrophobic and stinking conditions inside the shelter. The extent to which people would be able to continue to think and act rationally under these conditions is extremely limited.

Clearly, therefore, domestic residence PF values as produced by the Home Office are overestimated, but by how much is difficult to ascertain, in view of the unknown and variable factors outlined above. Studies in the USA take an average PF value of 5 or 6 for people in houses or buildings (for those in proper fallout shelters this rises to a PF of 10-40). Given the government's figures, the overall average PF in the UK would be 21. The *London After the Bomb* study calculated PFs after taking blast damage into account and their results are shown in Table 3.4.[23] These factors are clearly much lower than the government figures and are more in line with the US assumptions.

Table 3.4: Protection Factors after Allowing for Blast Damage

Zone	Blast Pressure (p.s.i.)	Protection Factors Lower value	Upper value
A	12	1	1
B	5–12	1	2
C	2–5	2	5
D	1–2	5	10

The lower values of protection factors represent a reasonable estimate once blast damage is taken into account. The upper value is optimistic and discounts the majority of blast damage. In Zone D the value of 10 corresponds to a Home Office calculated value for an undamaged house (*Domestic Nuclear Shelters: Technical Guidance*).
N.B. A PF of 1 implies no protection at all.

For many survivors, of course, the PF of a shelter is a largely academic matter since the houses that they lived in have been totally destroyed or so severely damaged as to afford no protection whatsoever. Exposure in the open air with radiation levels initially at 400 rads/hour would mean that within two hours a person would have absorbed enough radiation to be assured of prompt and painful death. Less time would be needed for the young, sick or elderly. Only an hour's exposure would mean that death would be very likely within the next two to three months.

Table 3.5 sets out the accumulated dose rates for initial dose rates of 1,000, 300 and 100 rads/hour. These are the typical dose rate contours for the explosion of a 10 MT weapon as illustrated by Glasstone and Dolan.[25] These accumulated doses are given over various periods of time

Table 3.5: Accumulated Radiation Doses

Time After Explosion (hours)	Relative† Dose Rate (rads/hr)	Accumulated Dose at Initial Dose Rate of*											
		1,000 r/h				300 r/h				100 r/h			
		N.P.	PF10	PF5	PF2	N.P.	PF10	PF5	PF2	N.P.	PF10	PF5	PF2
1	1	1,000	100	200	500	300	30	60	150	100	10	20	50
2	0.4	1,400	140	280	700	420	42	84	210	140	14	28	70
4	0.15	1,550	155	310	775	465	46	92	232	155	15	30	77
6	0.10	1,650	165	330	825	495	49	98	247	165	16	32	82
12	0.05	1,700	170	340	850	510	51	102	255	170	17	34	85
24 (1 day)	0.024	1,724	172	344	862	517	52	104	258	172	17	34	86
36	0.016	1,740	174	348	870	522	52	104	261	174	17	34	87
48 (2 days)	0.011	1,751	175	350	875	525	52	104	263	175	17	34	87
72 (3 days)	0.0062	1,757	175	350	878	527	53	106	264	175	17	34	87
100 (4+ days)	0.0036	1,761	176	352	880	528	53	106	264	176	18	36	88
200 (8+ days)	0.0017	1,763	176	352	881	529	53	106	265	176	18	36	88
500 (20+ days)	0.0005	1,764	176	352	882	529	53	106	265	176	18	36	88
1,000 (41+ days)	0.00023	1,764	176	352	882	529	53	106	265	176	18	36	88

N.P. = No protection
PF2 = Protection factor of 2
PF5 = Protection factor of 5
PF10 = Protection factor of 10
* All figures rounded to nearest whole figure
† Source of relative dose rate: *Nuclear Radiation in Warfare*,[24] Table 15, p. 81.

up to six weeks after the explosion and for persons with no protection as well as those inside buildings with PFs of 10, 5 and 2. These correspond approximately to the more optimistic figure – 10 – for undamaged houses in areas of light damage given by the government and the more realistic figure – 5 – given for blast-damaged houses in areas of light damage, and for blast-damaged houses in areas of moderate damage – 2. In areas of total destruction and heavy damage the protection factor of houses will be 1, i.e. no protection.

It can be clearly seen that with no protection in the 1,000 r/h initial dose rate zone sufficient radiation (600 rads +) will be accumulated to cause rapid death within the first hour but that in the 300 r/h zone, even after six weeks in the open, immediate (i.e. within two to three months) death would not be certain although certainly very probable. Death from cancer and related illnesses in the longer term would be virtually certain at such rates, however. In the 100 r/h zone, only a total of 176 rads are accumulated after six weeks in the open, and as Table 3.2 shows, whilst this will cause mild radiation sickness, it will on average not cause immediate death.

When the figures for PF10 and PF5 are examined, however, it can be seen that even the realistic figure of PF5 produces levels of only 106 rads and 36 rads after six weeks for the two smaller initial dose rates. Due to the rapid initial decay, levels are already reduced to 104 rads and 34 rads respectively after two days. The levels for the more optimistic figure of PF10 gives two day levels at 52 rads and 17 rads. Using the *London After the Bomb* study figure of a PF2 for houses in the zone of moderate blast damage it can be seen that at 1,000 r/h initial dose rate, immediate death is certain, at 300 r/h initial dose rate immediate death is possible but not likely, although long-term illness is very likely. At 100 r/h initial dose rate an accumulated dose of 88 rads after six weeks (87 rads after two days) is not enough to cause immediate death and less likely to cause severe illness in the long term.

In conclusion therefore it can be said that immediate death through accumulated doses of radiation is only likely to occur where people's homes have been totally destroyed or severely damaged. Otherwise the protection afforded by people's homes (with the exception of moderate damage in the 1,000 r/h area) in areas of moderate and light blast damage will be sufficient to prevent immediate death and will reduce the accumulated doses to relatively low amounts. As is pointed out in the BMA Report[20] however, the exact magnitude of the risk of developing cancer after exposure to radiation has not yet been quantified. The Japanese data show increases in many forms of cancer as well as cataracts and stillbirths. Even those exposed to a total dose rate of 5-19 rads have double the leukaemia rate of the general population. It has been estimated that 2-3 per cent of those people exposed to 100 rads will develop cancer.

Whilst some degree of protection against radiation is clearly afforded by people's homes, it must be pointed out that this assumes that the survivors were fit and healthy before the bomb was dropped, that an inner refuge has been constructed in the home and that the psychological stress associated with the situation has not prevented people from following the guidelines for their safety laid down by the government. Needless to say this protection will only occur outside of the zones of severe damage by blast and fire and away from the path of any moving fire-fronts.

References

1. Home Office, *Civil Defence Review*, Emergency Services Circular ES1/81 (HMSO, London, 1981).
2. D. Campbell, *War Plan U.K.* (Burnett Books, London, 1982).
3. Home Office, *Home Defence Planning Assumptions*, Emergency Services Circular ES3/73 (HMSO, London, 1973).
4. Draft Statutory Instrument, *Draft Civil Defence (General Local Authority Functions) Regulations 1983* (HMSO, London, 1983).
5. Draft Statutory Instrument, *Draft Civil Defence (Grant) (Amendment) Regulations 1983* (HMSO, London, 1983).
6. Draft Statutory Instrument, *The Civil Defence (Grant) (Scotland) Amendment Regulations 1983*.
7. Draft Statutory Instrument, *The Civil Defence (General Local Authority Functions) (Scotland) Regulations 1983* (HMSO, London, 1983).
8. Royal United Services Institute (ed.), *Nuclear Attack: Civil Defence* (Brassey's, Oxford, 1982).
9. P. Laurie, *Beneath the City Streets* (Granada Publishing, London, 1970; revised and updated, 1983).
10. Home Office, *Machinery of Government in War*, Emergency Services Circular ES7/73 (HMSO, London, 1973).
11. R. Hodgson and R. Banks, *Britain's Home Defence Gamble* (Conservative Political Centre, London).
12. Hansard, *House of Commons Debate 24 March 1983*, pp. 1088-1103.
13. Home Office, *Protection of the General Public in War*, Emergency Services Circular ES3/81 (HMSO, London, 1981).
14. Home Office Scientific Advisory Branch, *Protective Qualities of Buildings* (HMSO, London, 1981).
15. Home Office, *Protect and Survive* (HMSO, London, 1980).
16. Home Office, *Domestic Nuclear Shelters* (HMSO, London, 1981): advice on domestic shelters providing protection against nuclear explosions.
17. Home Office, *Water Services in War*, Emergency Services Circular ES6/76 (HMSO, London, 1976).

18. Home Office, *Food and Agriculture Controls in War*, Emergency Services Circular ES1/79 (HMSO, London, 1979).
19. A. Jackson, *Feeding the United Kingdom after a Nuclear Attack – a Preliminary Review* (Journal of the Institute of Civil Defence, October 1980).
20. British Medical Association's Board of Science and Education, *The Medical Effects of Nuclear War* (John Wiley & Sons, Chichester, 1983).
21. Home Office, *Environmental Health in War*, Emergency Services Circular ES8/76 (HMSO, London, 1976).
22. L. Godfrey, 'Seminar for Survival', *Protect and Survive Monthly* (May 1981).
23. LATB Study Group, *London After the Bomb* (Oxford University Press, Oxford, 1982).
24. Stockholm International Peace Research Institute, *Nuclear Radiation in Warfare* (Taylor & Francis, London, 1981).
25. S. Glasstone and P.J. Dolan (eds.), *The Effects of Nuclear Weapons* (United States Department of Energy: 3rd edition, Castle House, Tunbridge Wells, 1980).
26. Home Office and Scottish Home and Health Department, *Nuclear Weapons* (HMSO, London, 1974).
27. Greater London Council, *Greater London Housing Condition Survey, 1981* (London, 1981).

4 INCREASED INDIVIDUAL PROTECTION IN THE EVENT OF NUCLEAR WAR — NUCLEAR SHELTERS AND OTHER MEASURES

Should an individual not consider government advice adequate to protect his family in the event of nuclear war, what can he do?

Emigration to a safer part of the world or moving to a safer part of the UK are fairly drastic options given that few people consider nuclear war to be at all imminent. In addition, the question of deciding as to whether an area or country is 'safe' is not straightforward, in view of the problems of wind-blown radioactive fallout and the continual proliferation of nuclear weapons throughout the world.

Self-evacuation to a second home in a 'safe' area in the event of a threatened crisis is another available option, but this may well be prevented by the emergency rule of the day and in any event, substantial financial resources would be needed to maintain a second home as an option for retreat. The problems of deciding where is 'safe' are the same as above.

The third possibility, and one which has received much public attention, is that of providing one's own specifically designed shelter which would protect against all effects of nuclear attack. This could be provided within the curtilage of one's own property. Alternatively it may be possible to purchase a place in a larger shelter provided by either community or commercial enterprise. Very few such places are available at present, however. In both instances fairly substantial financial resources are needed to purchase such protection.

Given that an individual is unable to afford any of the above three measures, what, if anything, can be done to improve the protective quality of his existing accommodation?

This chapter will be considering what options are currently available for self-protection by an individual. It must be pointed out, however, that this self-protection is with respect to the short term only; whether or not this guarantees survival in the medium and long term after the explosion of a nuclear weapon will be discussed in Chapter 5.

The government has produced technical guidance[1] on the design and installation of nuclear shelters, giving practical details on the construction of four different types of shelter. A leaflet[2] summarising this advice has also been produced. Government guidance has been promised with regard to the variety of private shelters currently available commercially. Such guidance however is not yet available; nor have any of the consumer associations carried out any detailed appraisal of the currently available shelters – either those proposed by the government or those available commercially. An individual must therefore rely very much on his own judgement as to how much protection he needs, and how he should best provide it. Full protection against blast is very expensive to provide and if the house does not lie within a target area such protection is very unlikely to be needed; it is protection against fallout only that is required. In any case, nothing can provide guaranteed protection against a direct hit except several hundred feet of hard rock. An individual would therefore need to make some sort of judgement as to whether his home was in an area likely to be affected by blast and heat, or whether it was simply protection against fallout that he needed.

In the event of a full-scale attack of the order of 200-300 megatons, or even a counterforce attack, it is extremely likely that a large proportion of the UK population would be subjected to the effects of blast and heat. It can be seen from Table 2.1 on page 12 that severe blast damage (4 p.s.i. and over) extends for a radius of 5 miles around a 1 MT air-burst weapon, thus covering an area of 78.5 square miles. Assuming that 200 1 MT bombs fall without causing overlap in their zones of severe blast damage, then an area of 15,700 square miles of the most densely populated part of the UK would be subject to severe blast damage. Severe fire effects extend beyond the range of the blast effects and as can be seen from Table 2.7 (page 29), the range of third degree burns and spontaneous ignition of paper and fabrics is up to 14.5 miles from a 1 MT air-burst weapon. A total area of 132,037 square miles of the UK would thus be subject to severe fire and burns problems assuming that 200 separate 1 MT bombs are dropped in a large-scale or counterforce attack on the UK. However, if only a few bombs are dropped on the UK or bombs are dropped only on our neighbours on the European mainland, the majority of the population would require protection against the effects of fallout only. This is easier to provide than protection against blast and heat and even the simple precautions outlined in government publications, if followed, would be capable of saving millions of lives in the short term. As important as the provision of a fallout shelter, however, is an understanding of what radiation is and what it does to the human body, in order that people make sensible use of the fallout protection that is available to them. Since construction of the government-designed shelters requires considerable inputs of labour and materials, it will be impossible for many people to construct their own shelters; the elderly, sick, infirm and many other individuals who for various reasons could not move large amounts of earth (assuming they had a garden – 6 per cent of the housing stock in the UK comprises flats of five storeys or more), or bricks or concrete blocks. In time of crisis there may well develop shortages of the materials commonly required to provide additional protection, and the government may well have to requisition many of the available supplies for emergency work. Purchase of a private shelter which would be constructed within the curtilage of one's own home requires substantial financial resources as well as, in most cases, a garden.

In view of these limitations, therefore, the only way for many people to increase their protection is to improve the protective capacity of the house in which they are currently living. This option will therefore be examined in detail before consideration is given to purpose-built shelters.

Improving the Protective Capacity of a House

Whilst the houses in an area may well differ in their design and construction, they will need to withstand largely identical forces of blast and heat as well as afford protection against radioactive fallout. Obviously some houses will provide far better protection than others – in general, older houses with thicker walls, heavier roofs and smaller windows will afford better protection against blast, fire and fallout than more modern housing with thinner walls containing large areas of glazing and lightweight panels. Mid-terrace houses and large detached or semi-detached houses will provide more protection from fallout than small bungalows or caravans. The protection offered by the latter two is in fact so minimal that the government relaxes its stay-at-home instructions for these residents and urges them to arrange to shelter with someone nearby. Short of moving, however, there is little that can be done about the basic design and construction of a house in the immediate crisis period before a hostile attack.

Protection Against Blast

The blastwave can cause severe damage or totally destroy houses depending on the size of the exploded weapon and the distance from the explosion. There is nothing to be done to prevent this total destruction since no amount of strengthening or supporting will enable the building to resist the enormous overpressures and winds blowing at several hundred miles per hour. For example when a 1 MT bomb has been exploded, there will be winds of up to 1,600 mph for a mile from the explosion, falling to 400 mph at 2 miles, 130 mph at 5 miles and 50 mph at 10 miles. Winds at this lowest limit are sufficient to cause minor structural damage in the UK; the effects of the higher wind-speeds have never been experienced in this country but the massive destruction can be imagined. Any house in this area is more than likely to be knocked flat or have only one or two walls remaining. The house can provide no protection against the following fallout and there can be little hope of any survivors being dug out from the debris. The only 'safe' option in this case is not to be inside the house at the time of the explosion. Damage such as this would extend up to 2.5 miles from a ground-burst 1 MT explosion or 3.75 miles from an air-burst 1 MT explosion, covering areas of 19.6 and 44.2 square miles respectively.[3]

Beyond these zones of total destruction and severe damage, the effects of the blastwave continue to lessen until eventually there is no damage at all. In the area of moderate and light damage, however, there will still be considerable damage to people's homes although they will, by and large, remain standing. Roof tiles will be stripped as well as windows and doors blown in and there will be some cracks in the masonry depending on quality of construction and materials used. These areas of lesser damage would extend up to 8.75 miles from a 1 MT ground-burst or 15 miles from a 1 MT air-burst bomb, covering areas of 240 and 706 square miles respectively.[3] Again there is very little that can be done to prevent the damage occurring: blocking up doors and windows with concrete blocks, planks of wood and heavy furniture will prevent them blowing in, thus reducing the area through which fallout can penetrate into the house and also providing protection against the extensive damage that can be caused to human bodies by flying glass.

In summary, therefore, there is very little that a householder can do to protect his home against the effects of the blastwave; the only protection in the more severely damaged areas is to avoid being in the house at all. Even in houses with only light blast damage, the dangers from fallout will have been greatly increased due to the openings that have been created in the buildings through which lethal fallout will blow.

Protection Against Fire

The intense heatwave which follows virtually immediately after the explosion, precedes the blastwave by a matter of seconds. This heatwave was not experienced in the UK in the Second World War since the bombs used were not capable of producing such effects; only nuclear weapons are capable of creating such massive waves of heat. The heat-wave itself will pass in a matter of seconds, but widespread damage will be caused, or at least started, during these few brief seconds. Unlike the blastwave, which has little direct effect on human beings (except where the high winds blow them into things, causing mechanical injury and death), the heatwave will cause potentially lethal burns on any exposed human flesh for many miles from the point of explosion. In addition it causes direct damage to houses. The range of damage for the heatwave is more extensive than that for blast damage – third degree burns and spontaneous ignition of paper and fabrics will occur up to eight miles from a 1 MT air-burst explosion whereas severe blast damage extends for only five miles.

A far greater number of householders therefore will be concerned with the effects of fire and, unlike the blastwave, there are some precautions that can be taken by the householder to minimise its effects. These precautions are only possible at some distance from the point of explosion, however; in nearer areas the very intensity of the heat will prevent any possible action having an effect whatsoever. As is shown in Table 2.7, up to 2.2 miles from an air-burst 1 MT weapon most substances, including human bodies and many building materials as well as metals, will vaporise. No precautions can safeguard against such massive amounts of heat.

Likewise, no precautions can be taken that will prevent damage to a house that is within the area covered by a fire-storm or is in the path of a moving fire-front. As with severe blast damage, the only form of protection for someone who lives in such areas is not to be in the house at the time of explosion. The area over which fire-storms are likely to develop is not known with any certainty, although it is unlikely that this will extend beyond the zone of severe blast damage; therefore only those houses which are reduced to rubble are likely also to be reduced to ashes in mass fires. In the fringe around the zone of severe blast damage, i.e. in the 3 miles between the 5- and 8-mile damage limits mentioned above, there are a number of precautions that the house-holder can take to reduce the damage by fire that is likely to occur. Most of these precautions would need to be taken in advance of the explosion, however, since considerable time would be needed for some of the preparations.

Since the heatwave only ignites things that it touches, an obvious precaution is to remove anything which is easily ignited or which burns easily. This applies to items outside the house as well as items inside. Due to shielding effects, it is more likely that upper rooms would be subject to the effects of the heatwave. Since it is only through windows or open doors that the heatwave penetrates (it cannot shine through walls), an obvious precaution is to prevent the heatwave from entering by keeping doors closed and coating any glazed areas with white paint to reflect the heatwave. Since the blastwave will break all windows in areas where there is danger from the heatwave, even these precautions are useless if there is more than one explosion, since the blastwave of the first will permit entry of the heatwave in second and subsequent cases, unless windows and other openings have been very strongly boarded up.

Other precautions mentioned in the government leaflet[4] include instructions to:

— remove net curtains or thin materials from windows;
— clean out old newspapers and magazines;
— keep a fire extinguisher to hand;
— keep buckets of water ready on each floor;
— keep any remaining doors closed to help prevent the spread of fire;
— turn off gas and electricity at mains, together with gas pilot lights and oil supplies.

Without doubt all these precautions will be of value in helping to prevent fire spreading if only one or two small blazes are started by the heatwave. It is impossible, however, for the majority of households to put out many small fires or even one or two larger fires given the rapid rate of burning of modern furniture, and the toxic fumes given off. It is very much a matter of chance which houses are shielded against the heatwave effects, since the source of explosion cannot be known in advance.

In summary, it must be said that the householder can do very little about the fire hazards if he is within five miles of the typical 1 MT explosion. The heat is so intense as to defy normal precautions. Beyond this, however, sensible precautions will reduce the chances of individual houses catching fire.

Protection Against Fallout

This is the effect of nuclear war which has been most discussed. It is also the effect against which most people's homes afford some protection. The extent to which individual homes provide protection was described in detail in Chapter 3. What can the householder do, if any-thing, to improve his protection? It was shown in Chapter 3 that people's homes do afford some degree of protection against radiation in zones of moderate and light damage, as well as areas where there has been no blast or fire damage at all. Strict adherence to government guidelines, especially with regard to the correct construction of a refuge room, and having thoroughly prepared equipment and provisions will reduce the likely accumulated dose of radiation to a non-lethal dose for a fit and healthy individual. Increased protection can be provided by increasing the thickness of material around the inner refuge rooms, the greatest protection being afforded by the most dense materials, and by ensuring that sufficient arrangements have been made to avoid the necessity of leaving the shelter before radiation levels had dropped to the 'safe' dose.

The individual however is dependent on the government giving suffi-cient and correct warning of any hostile attack, which it may well not be able to do if the electromagnetic pulse has destroyed the com-munications systems.

Provision of Purpose-built Shelter Protection — Government Shelter Designs

A manual of technical guidance on the design of domestic nuclear shelters was published by the government in 1981,[1] together with a leaflet giving less detailed information.[2] These had been prepared by a working party set up by the Emergency Services Division of the Home Office and comprise two parts:

— technical guidance for professional engineers to assist them in pro-ducing reliable shelter designs
— detailed designs of five shelters, applicable to different sorts of house and price ranges

Types 1a and 1b are improvised designs to be built in the garden at short notice; they will give little protection against blast and are designed primarily for fallout protection. Type 2 is an indoor shelter, a variation in fact on the Second World War Morrison shelter, designed to sustain the debris load resulting from complete collapse of a normal two-storey house as well as to provide protection against fallout. Type 3 is an outdoor shelter to be built from a manufactured kit to be semi-sunk in the ground and covered with earth: it would provide both blast and fallout protection. Type 4 is a permanent purpose-built shelter made of reinforced concrete which has to be built by professionals. If correctly constructed it is designed to provide a high degree of protection against both blast and radiation.

General guidance is provided in addition to the more technical guidance for professional engineers. A summary of these general design requirements is set out below in order to show the various aspects of life in a shelter which need to be considered:

Space Requirements

Minimum requirements in a sealed family shelter are

– volume per person	65 cubic feet (1.8 cubic metres)
– total volume	400 cubic feet (11.3 cubic metres)
– floorspace/person	10 square feet (1.0 square metres)
– total floorspace	65 square feet (6.0 square metres)
– headroom	6 feet 6 inches (2 metres)

These requirements are limited primarily by the need to have sufficient ventilation for the occupants.

Ventilation and Filtration

In a sealed shelter (i.e. with a permanent door closure) there must be a fan or pump capable of delivering a minimum of 3 cubic feet of air (1.4 litres per second) for each person in the shelter. If more than adequate capacity is installed it will avoid the need for continual operation – for example, a fan with a capacity of 3 litres per second need be operated for only 30 minutes in every hour. Air filters should be attached to the fan mechanism to prevent radioactive dust particles from entering the shelter.

Any fan would need to be shut down

– immediately following attack (to prevent filters clogging with dust)
– in the event of nearby external fires (to prevent dangerous fumes being drawn in)
– when fallout is expected to arrive (notification by radio)

The fan cannot be switched off for long, however, before dangerous levels of carbon dioxide begin to build up. A dangerous level of 4 per cent will be built up in the minimum size shelter containing 4 people in 6½ hours; if there are 6 people this figure will be reduced to 4½ hours.

Any ventilation system should:

— change the air in the shelter at least three times every hour
— include an air-intake route that is tortuous rather than direct
— include a dust trap
— provide alternative motivating power
— be either an intake system, drawing in fresh air, or an extractor, expelling the stale air.

Sanitation

Special sanitation arrangements will be necessary because there will be no water to waste in flush toilets; some form of chemical toilet will be necessary. Some of those currently on the market can be used for a number of days without producing unpleasant smells. At some point, however, the contents of the toilet will need to be put outside the shelter.

Exit and Entrance

All entrances, escape hatches and ventilation pipes should be as far as possible from nearby buildings – at least one half the height of the nearest building. This is to avoid as far as possible any debris from damaged buildings or blown down trees blocking means of exit or entry and sources of air supply. All points of entry must be correctly designed to withstand the blast pressure. Any door should always open out to ensure that the blast overpressure is more safely distributed across the entrance. At least one door should be removable from the inside in order to aid escape.

Shelter Supplies

Extensive lists of shelter supplies are provided in the various publications concerned with survival in the shelter.[4,1,5,6] The most important of the shelter supplies is water. Two pints per head per day are essential for survival but more will be needed for sanitation: 3½-4 pints is generally recommended, although it may be necessary to store these outside of the shelter (provided the containers are adequately sealed, the contents will not become contaminated by radioactivity).

Food stocks should be selected on the basis that they keep a long time without refrigeration, are easily prepared and require little or no cooking. Suggested[1] foodstocks for one person for two weeks are:

Biscuits, crackers, breakfast cereals, etc.	2750 g
Tinned meat or fish (e.g. tinned beef, luncheon meat, stewed steak, pilchards, sardines)	2000 g
Tinned vegetables (e.g. baked beans, carrots, potatoes, sweetcorn, etc.).	1800 g
Tinned margarine or butter, or peanut butter	500 g
Jam, marmalade, honey or spread	500 g
Tinned soup	6 tins
Full cream evaporated milk (or dried milk)	14 small tins (2 x 300 g containers)
Sugar	700 g
Tea or coffee (instant)	250 g
Boiled sweets or other sweets	450 g
Tinned fruit, fruit juices, fruit squash, drinking chocolate	If sufficient storage space is available

Other supplies which would be important in maintaining some semblance of civilised life include the following:

Portable radio (receiving medium wave) and spare batteries. A spare radio would be desirable for underground shelters. It is essential to have a radio with an aerial socket. A makeshift aerial can be fitted up passing to the outside of the shelter. A socket on the radio is then necessary to receive the connection to the aerial.

Tin opener, bottle opener, cutlery and crockery

Warm clothing and changes of clothing

Bedding, sleeping bags, etc.

Saucepans, food containers

Torches with spare bulbs and batteries

Toilet articles, toilet rolls, plastic buckets

Overalls or an outdoor coat which can be left near the shelter entrance in case you have to go outside the shelter.

First aid kit and simple remedies

Box of dry sand, cloths or tissues for wiping plates and utensils

Notebooks and pencils

Games, toys, magazines

Clock (mechanical) and calendar

Sanitation supplies such as polythene bag linings, strong disinfectant

Two dustbins or buckets, one for temporary storage of sealed bags of waste matter and one for food remains, empty tins and rubbish.

This is a very basic list. Given more room in a specially designed shelter, Sibley[6] suggests that the following items may be of use during and after the shelter period

— flash light and signal lamps
— campers cooking stoves
— walkie-talkie transmitters
— dose meters
— compressed air cylinders
— maps
— electric cable
— rope and string
— packets of seeds
— large water tank
— pick-axes, spades, forks, sledge hammers
— wire cutters, hammer, saw, nails, screws, screwdrivers
— small arms, rifles, shotguns, etc. and ammunition

This last item would be primarily used for killing dangerous and possibly diseased packs of wild animals. Sadly, they may also be used to protect man against man, when the civilised veneer has been removed by the horrors of nuclear war.

Protection Afforded by Government-designed Shelters

Type 1a: Easily-constructed Improvised Garden Shelter using Household Materials

This shelter comprises a shallow trench dug into the ground with a roof of doors or other timber, supported above ground level by earth walls, with a covering of 18 ins. of earth. It has no fitted door and the entrance is closed by means of a barrier of sand-bags or packed soil. It is unsuitable in areas where there is a high water table. This is designed to withstand overpressures of 1.5 p.s.i. The LATB study group[7] found that if there was an attack on London (on the scale practised in the Square Leg exercise) such shelters would collapse over more than 85 per cent of the GLC area. The majority of houses in the UK withstand overpressures of up to 4 p.s.i., albeit somewhat damaged. A radiation protective factor of 40 is claimed — this would be an impossible claim in the 85 per cent of cases where the shelter has been destroyed, since there would then be no protection at all against the radiation.

Whilst this form of shelter would be unlikely to catch fire itself, it would offer no protection at all in the event of any mass fires developing in the vicinity. It is estimated to take 48 man hours to construct, but it would be impossible for many of the population to do so, either because of inability or lack of suitable space.

Type 1b: Improvised Outdoor Shelter using DIY Materials

This shelter likewise comprises a shallow trench dug in the ground over which a frame of scaffold poles is constructed and covered with plywood boarding and the whole thing covered in polythene before being covered with 18 ins. of earth. Again there is no sealed entrance and small sandbags should be placed in the opening. There is the added refinement of a metal drainpipe forming provision for extra ventilation. 48 man hours and DIY materials would be needed for its construction. Unless purchased well in advance it would be surprising if such materials would be available in large quantities in any recognised crisis period.

As with Type 1a it is claimed to be able to withstand 1.5 overpressures. The limited protection of this capacity was outlined above. With the unsealed entrance there is no question of it withstanding any mass fires. A PF factor of 40 similar to the Type 1a shelter is claimed. This is likewise only valid if the shelter remains intact, which with a blast protection factor of 1.5 it is not very likely to do.

Type 2: Indoor Shelter from Manufactured Kit

This shelter – very much akin to the Second World War Morrison shelter – comprises a protective steel table which can be erected in homes that have basements or rooms that can be converted into fallout rooms (providing the floor is strong enough to support it). It is designed to provide protection in the event of the complete collapse of a normal two-storey building. It should not be used in houses that have more than two storeys, on upper floors; in blocks of flats of precast concrete panel construction or which have load-bearing brickwork on the top two floors of a block of flats, or in lightly clad buildings. In order for it to provide any fallout protection, however, it must be surrounded with bricks, sand, heavy furniture, etc. as per instructions in *Protect and Survive*[4] for hiding under the stairs. It is claimed to be able to withstand a force of 6 p.s.i.; since an overpressure of 5 p.s.i. will destroy most houses in the UK, however, it will provide protection against the collapse of buildings on people sheltering in their homes. Since it relies on natural ventilation, the entrance must be left open at all times; it would not provide any additional protection in the event of fire since smoke and fumes will penetrate into the shelter. A PF factor of 70 is claimed against the effects of radiation; this would really only apply when the house around it is still standing, since the open entrance will provide easy access for radioactive dust. Clearly, if the house is largely undamaged the steel box will help reduce the radiation levels for its occupants. The great advantage in the use of such shelters in the Second World War was, of course, that if the house did collapse it was simply a matter of waiting for someone to come and dig you out of the protective steel box. In the event of a nuclear attack the problems of fire and fallout would prevent anyone being dug out.

Type 3: Outdoor Shelter from a Manufactured Kit

This type of shelter is suitable where there is a garden with the house. It consists of a strong structural shell with prefabricated steel components bolted together to form a sealed room large enough for six people (cramped) or four (comfortable). It is semi-sunk in the ground and covered entirely by earth. The excavation would probably take a week for two people digging by hand. This is similar to the Anderson shelter used in the Second World War but it is sealed and provided with a blast door and escape hatches.

Blast protection is claimed for up to 11 p.s.i. overpressure. The ability to withstand such tremendous forces is achieved by the flexibility of the shell which yields until the surrounding earth compacts sufficiently to deflect the blast wave around the shell, although there may be permanent damage and distortion to the shell. Protection against 11 p.s.i. would give protection as close as three miles from ground zero of a 1 MT air burst. This is well within the zone likely to suffer the most severe heat effects and no indication is given as to the likely effects of fire on the shelter. It may well be that the metal and ventilation pipes and external doors would melt or distort at the high temperatures. Table 2.7 (page 29) shows that metals would be liable to melting up to 3½ miles from ground zero of a 1 MT air-burst explosion. A protection factor of not less than 200 is claimed for this shelter which is surprising given that the government also notes that the fallout protection provided depends on the depth of earth covering the shelter. From diagrams this would appear to be no more than that covering the improvised Type 1 shelters with their PF of 40. The difference is presumably accounted for by the fact that the shelter is sealed with forced ventilation rather than relying on natural ventilation.

Type 4: Permanent Purpose-built Shelter

This is a reinforced concrete shelter which must be built by a specialist contractor, unlike the other three types which could be built by a reasonably strong 'handy' person. Access to a rear garden would clearly be required for such a shelter, which would need to be constructed during peacetime. The government claims a PF of 300 and a blast protection in excess of 11 p.s.i. This protection stems from the density of material used, the reinforcement of roof, floor and walls and the amount of earth surrounding the structure.

A second room used as a decontamination chamber is incorporated. This shelter design is broadly comparable to the shelters that are currently available commercially and will be examined in more detail below when the other commercial shelters are considered.

Private Shelters for Purchase

The early 1980s saw a rapid boom in the production of private family shelters. A number of firms have recently entered the home shelter field although some have already ceased trading. There has as yet been no government control or regulation imposed upon this new commercial activity and as Alley[8] notes, there are abuses; advertising claims may be misleading, designs and products may be inadequate. A survey of some of the shelters currently available commercially was carried out by L. Godfrey and published in the *Observer* Magazine on 4 July 1982.[9] Godfrey points out that although the business potential had attracted several hundred optimistic firms, there had been only a few hundred sales throughout the British Isles. This he attributed to the high cost of effective protection and the well-justified caution of the prospective customers.

Most of these custom-built shelters are designed to provide protection against both blast and fallout. Since most urban areas would be completely destroyed by blast overpressures of 5-10 p.s.i. any shelter providing protection greater than 10 p.s.i. can be considered a blast shelter. No mention is made of protection against the effects of heat and fire. Information was obtained from as many firms as possible although many firms were reluctant to provide information for the purposes of comparative research. The main facts about each of the shelters are set out in Table 4.1. Names of the respective firms have been omitted.

Table 4.1: Commercial Nuclear Shelters

Firm	Construction	Depth of Burial	Size	Entrance, Exit & Ventilation	Claimed PF Against Fallout	Claimed Resistance to Blast	Price (excluding VAT) (March 1983)
A	2 chamber stainless steel (0.06") cylindrical shelter	Semi-submerged	7'0" x 14'9" (6 person)	Entrance to main chamber – 3'3" diam. raised neck access with dished cover opening outwards. 2nd entrance with aluminium ladder. 2 emergency escape covers.	200+	11 p.s.i.	£4,984 (excl. installation) No fittings included
B	2 chamber steel (0.2" steelplate) cylindrical structures based on underground petrol storage tanks	42" below ground level	9' x 12' for 4 person (160 ft³ per person)	2 vertical shafts protected by 2 covers. Ventilation shafts have steel covers & are fitted with filter units (battery driven & manual unit for back-up).	10,000	150 p.s.i.	£4,150 – 4 person £7,364 – 24 person. Price includes radio, scintillation counter, protective suiting, dosimeters, bunkbeds, food & installation. Other equipment will be supplied on demand giving a total of £6,336.40 for 4 persons & £15,276.40 for 24 persons
C Type 1	2 chamber reinforced concrete – 10" thick walls & 12" thick roof	20" below ground level	85 cubic ft per person	2 heavy caste blast doors for entrance & escape hatch with protective grills.	4,000	15 p.s.i.	£9,000 (5 person) to £19,000 (15 person)

Table 4.1: Contd.

Firm	Construction	Depth of Burial	Size	Entrance, Exit & Ventilation	Claimed PF Against Fallout	Claimed Resistance to Blast	Price (excluding VAT) (March 1983)
Type 2	2 chamber reinforced concrete – 12" thick walls, 18" floor & 20" thick roof	20" below ground level	ditto	ditto	8,000	45 p.s.i.	£10,000 (5 person) to £22,000 (15 person) excl. installation
D	2 chamber 6"-8" thick precast reinforced concrete	24" below ground level	6 person 290 ft³ ea. 8 person 262 ditto 10 person 280 ditto	2 airtight hatches protect entrance & escape hatch. Ventilation & filters fitted	2,500 (3,300 if 12" layer of concrete is paved around shelter)	15 p.s.i.	£6,000 – 6 person. £14,000 – 14 person excl. installation
E Type 1	2 chamber cylindrical shelter of ¼" thick steelplate surrounded by 12" concrete	36" below ground level	8'9" x 12'9" 6 person 8'9" x 58'8" 39 person	Single access & exit via steel & concrete airtight hatch. Emergency escape route provided. Vent. & filter system fitted	1,000	15 p.s.i.	£17,000 for 6 person – £32,000 for 39 person incl. equipment and food
Type 2	2 chamber cylindrical shelter of 0.4" thick steel surrounded by 12" concrete	ditto	10' x 16'1" for 6 person to 10' x 62' for 39 person	ditto	2,000	45 p.s.i.	£24,000 for 6 person – £47,000 for 39 person incl. equipment and food

Table 4.1: Contd.

Firm	Construction	Depth of Burial	Size	Entrance, Exit & Ventilation	Claimed PF Against Fallout	Claimed Resistance to Blast	Price (excluding VAT) (March 1983)
F Type 1	2 chamber prefab. galvanised corrugated steel cylinders 0.1" thick walls	14' below ground level	8'6" x 16'5"	2 vertical shafts provide access & there are also 2 ventilation ducts	2,000+	45 p.s.i.	£9,658 excluding installation and equipment
Type 2	Single chamber shelter of prefab. galvanised corrugated steel cylinder walls 0.1" thick	Semi-submerged with 6' earth cover	9'8" x 7'2"	Single access & emergency escape via demountable panel	not stated	not stated	£3,500 excluding installation and equipment
Type 3	ditto	ditto	6'5" x 7'2"	Single access & ventilation via crawl tube	not stated	not stated	£2,500 excluding installation and equipment
Type 4	Galv. steel tubes & sheets for DIY	ditto	not stated	ditto	not stated	not stated	£1,000 in kit form, excluding installation and equipment
Type 5	Bolt together DIY kit for reinforcing on existing room or garage	above ground	adjustable	ditto	not stated	not stated	varies according to size
Govt. design	2 chamber reinforced concrete	Min of 12" of earth cover (increased protection at greater depth)	2.94 m x 4.15 m	2 air shafts but no filtration. Pump or hand-operated ventilation, single access & escape hatch provided in walls	300+	11 p.s.i.+	£6,000 – 10,000 – 4 persons (1980 prices)

From examination of the details submitted by the firms, which varied from rudimentary photocopied handouts to pseudo-scientific glossy brochures, the main impression was that claims for the protection offered were largely unsubstantiated (although not necessarily incorrect) and were necessarily dependent upon the correct behaviour of the potential occupants before, during and after a hostile attack. Blast protection would of course only be available if the occupants were actually sealed inside the shelter at the time of attack and the shelter would therefore offer no protection in the event of a surprise attack. Claims for similar structures often showed surprisingly large discrepancies and in some designs scant attention seemed to have been paid to the weakness of all shelter designs, i.e. the position and structure of entry hatches and ventilation shafts. Likewise, with the exception of one firm, the effects of the heatwave were not mentioned.

Since the claims of the manufacturers can be neither substantiated nor denied with any accuracy, a purchaser is being asked effectively to gamble relatively large sums of money in buying a product, the reliability of which will have to be taken on faith, since in the nature of events it will be impossible to claim redress from the manufacturer after the product has been used, i.e. after a nuclear war.

Cost of Private Shelters

The costs for the shelters, including the government shelter, vary, the average being between £1,000 and £2,000 per space for the buried shelters providing both blast and fallout protection. This however usually represents only the basic cost of the shelter plus access and ventilation systems; additional costs often include fittings, equipment and installation in the purchaser's garden; typical fittings and equipment for these shelters are protective clothing, food, water containers and filters, chemical toilet and other sanitation supplies, batteries, dose meters, fitted radio, electric fans and filters, and manually operated back-up systems (often included in price), generators, lighting, shower unit (for decontamination), scintillation meters, bunk beds, mattresses and blankets, sink and cooker units, bottled gas, pick and shovel, medical supplies and storage racks. A family of four could therefore reasonably expect to spend in the order of at least £10,000 in total.

In addition to private sources of finance to fund this purchase, it is possible that funding may be sought from building societies on the grounds that installation of a nuclear shelter could be considered a home improvement, increasing the value of the property. The 15 largest building societies in the country were approached to establish current policy and practice with regard to this matter. The four main areas of enquiry were: (i) whether the society had any agreed policy regarding funding of nuclear protection installations; (ii) whether the society had received applications for loans for this purpose; (iii) whether the proposed shelter design was assessed for suitability or if an approved list of suppliers was maintained; (iv) the extent to which money would be made available for such applications. Only two of the societies failed to respond to these queries, and the response received from the other 13 building societies as well as leading banks and the Building Societies Association was remarkable in its similarity.

None of the societies had an agreed policy on the subject of loans for nuclear shelters and said that each case would be dealt with on its merits as with other home improvements. Two societies said specifically that they were waiting for further guidance from the government before deciding on any specific policy.

Eight of the societies said that to their knowledge they had received no applications at all, while no more than 40 enquiries in total had been received by the other five societies, and a much smaller number of these enquiries had eventually materialised into loans.

No society had a list of approved suppliers and would not be in a position to warrant the suitability of the shelter for the purpose required of it. Lack of any suitable yardstick from the government was pointed out. Several of the societies noted that they were lending against the value of the whole property and were not particularly bothered by the details of the construction of such improvements.

The purchase of a nuclear shelter was considered as any other home improvement and money would be made available on the usual basis with repayment over the balance of the existing mortgage.

The overall response therefore could be summarised as that building societies would be willing to consider funding nuclear shelters should they receive any applications to do so and would treat them in the same way as any other home improvement their mortgagees might wish to make.

Effectiveness of Private Shelters

As stated above, the claimed effectiveness of a private shelter, against both blast and fallout, cannot be determined with any accuracy, and, due to the very nature of its function, it cannot be adequately tested prior to sale in order to ascertain a reliable estimate of its protective capacities. It can be seen from Table 4.1, however, that widely varying claims for similar structures have been made and claims should therefore be approached with a certain degree of caution.

All shelters however have potential problems and weaknesses inherent in their design which may limit their effectiveness. In addition, assumptions have to be made regarding effective warning and human behaviour in determining the protective capacity of any shelter; these problems and assumptions are examined below.

Most of the design problems are due to the fact that the majority of the private shelters commercially available are designed for burial underground. Since this is an essential aspect of their design, with the earth cover providing a large percentage of the fallout protection factor, it is necessary to try to mitigate these problems as far as possible.

One of the major problems with underground burial in the UK is water seepage into the shelter itself. Waterproofing techniques are employed wherever possible and high standards of workmanship are required in the construction of the shelter in order to obtain as high a level of watertightness as possible. Often it is necessary to assume that leakages will occur and provide a sump at the lowest level to enable water to collect. Automatic and hand pumps should be provided in this case. The government[1] specifies that all concrete used in underground shelters should have a strength of 30N per mm^2 at 28 days and should be vibrated to produce a dense watertight concrete. In the case of steel structures underground, the majority of designs available are cylindrical in order to provide maximum strength. These cylinders normally comprise several segments welded together: the joints between segments are susceptible to water leakage and considerable attention has to be paid to ensuring a completely watertight seal both before and after installation. Water seepage is a common problem and whilst it will not actually reduce the protection afforded by the shelter, it would make occupation of the shelter at the least uncomfortable and at the worst virtually impossible. Health problems would only be exacerbated by a damp, putrid atmosphere. This is one area, however, where a supplier (if still in business) can be called upon to correct any faults.

Another problem with burial underground is that of emergence following a nuclear attack. Entrance and exit hatches may be distorted by the blast and heatwaves and prove unopenable. Considerable amounts of heavy debris from fallen buildings may also have fallen across the site of the shelter making it impossible to get out. There could be no expectation of being dug out from outside. The government recommends[1] that all shelters of whatever design should be a minimum distance from the house (at least half the height of the house – measured to the eaves) in order to avoid the problems associated with debris being scattered above the shelter site. Likewise a shelter should not be placed near trees since the winds associated with the blastwave can easily uproot and blow over the largest of trees. In many designs escape hatches are placed in the side of the shelter through which, in cases where the usual access is blocked, a family could dig its way to the surface. The hatches, however, represent a structural weakness as well as providing an opportunity for water leakage into the shelter. Picks and shovels need to be kept in the shelter for this purpose.

Since all currently available shelters are entered from the surface (i.e. none provide a tunnel access from the house), it is necessary to provide at least one access route from ground level down into the shelter (many shelters do in fact provide two). These have to be kept covered and sealed against blast, heat and fallout, with which they will be in immediate contact. The ability of the hatches to withstand the tremendous forces imposed by the nuclear explosion is extremely questionable. All are constructed of metal; as Table 2.7 on page 29 showed, metals will vaporise up to 2.2 miles from a 1 MT explosion and melt up to 3.5 miles away. Since the hatches cannot be covered themselves by earth or concrete they are exposed to the full force of the blastwave and the high-speed winds associated with it. While their ability to do so cannot be verified or disproved without full-scale trials, it would seem unlikely that metal hatches fastened with hinges would be able to resist the forces unleashed by a nuclear explosion. Once the outer hatches have been destroyed, the protection against fallout will inevitably be reduced since fallout would be blown or carried by rain into the access chamber. This is, however, in most designs, divided from the main living chamber by a steel door which can be shut tightly. The access chamber is designed for use as a decontamination room after trips to and from the surface and contains the chemical toilet and waste products, making living conditions inside the main chamber more bearable. Once this second chamber is open to the elements, life inside the shelter is restricted to the single chamber and would become increasingly unpleasant, since the occupants would be confined to the single chamber; the protection against fallout would also be reduced.

A further problem inherent in the very nature of the shelter is that of the provision of adequate ventilation. Since the shelter must be effectively sealed in order to increase the protection it affords, it is necessary to have some form of forced ventilation. The required amounts of air per person were set out on page 81 above and this must be provided by a pump worked either automatically or by hand. An automatic ventilation system would be operated either by mains electricity, batteries or a generator. Any generator used, however, must be sited outside the living area of the shelter and must be supplied with its own ventilation and exhaust. Since mains electricity could be expected to fail within minutes of the explosion this clearly cannot be relied upon to provide the necessary ventilation. Whatever pumping system is used, the source of air will have to be that air (contaminated by radioactive particles) which lies outside the shelter, above ground. This is pumped down into the shelter through air intakes. It is vital that these are not blocked by debris since they represent the only source of air available to the shelter occupants. The government recommends[1] that air intakes should be at least 18 ins. above ground and sited where least damage would be expected from debris. A cowl should be fitted over the top of the intake to prevent debris and dust falling into it. Whether a relatively fragile structure such as a narrow tube standing 18 ins. above ground would be able to withstand the high-speed winds carrying heavy debris is certainly open to question, if not doubt.

Filters need to be fitted into the air intake shafts to ensure that the radioactive particles are filtered out. These will eventually become clogged, especially in the case of a ground-burst explosion, and supplies of replacement filters will need to be kept in the shelter. In addition to these problems, inherent in the design of any shelter, there is the problem of fire. There is virtually no mention at all in either government or commercial information regarding the protection that the various shelters provide against the effects of fire. It is however widely assumed[10,11,12] that any shelters lying within the area covered by a fire-storm would have all the oxygen drawn out of the shelter by the tremendous forces operating within the fire-storm, thereby causing death by asphyxiation for all persons in the shelter. Even areas where there is no actual fire-storm could experience very high temperatures (possibly exceeding $2,000°F$) and these, together with the production of carbon monoxide and other noxious fumes, would very possibly kill many of those sheltering below ground in their airtight containers.

A further problem which limits the effectiveness of blast shelters is that of the provision of warning of attack. The blast shelters will only offer protection against blast if the occupants are sealed within them at the moment of explosion. It would be impossible for anyone to reach the safety of their shelter in the few seconds between the moment of explosion and the arrival of the blastwave. Everyone, however, is entirely dependent upon the government to provide adequate warning. As stated earlier, this would only be of the order of 3-4 minutes in any case, which does not provide much time for a family to run the length of the garden, open hatches, climb down into the shelter and seal it behind themselves. If the warning system has been put out of action by the electromagnetic pulse there would of course be no warning at all. Even in periods of tension, it is unlikely that families would wish to spend the entire time sealed in their shelter on the offchance of an attack.

All of the blast shelters commercially available would provide complete protection against fallout providing the necessary precautions against contamination were taken, that sufficient provisions had been stored in the shelter and that the ventilation and filtration systems continued to work. If a hostile attack were spread out over a matter of weeks, however, supplies of water and food in even the most well-stocked of shelters would be extremely stretched to meet the needs of the occupants. Long occupancy also brings with it many problems. Inability to control temperature or humidity will cause discomfort and affect health, elementary sanitation will become increasingly difficult as time passes, and uncollected refuse and faecal material will encourage disease. Those who have received high radiation doses will show signs of sickness, and infections unrelated to radiation sickness will spread amongst occupants in the shelter. As noted by SIPRI,[12] the psychological stress caused by being forced to witness severe pain and death of dearly loved relatives, by worrying about missing family, by the stench of shelter life, will lead to social stresses and possibly violent or aggressive behaviour. In addition there may well be problems in keeping people out of the shelter – installation of an underground shelter could not go unnoticed by even the least inquisitive of neighbours – and since all shelters have a strict limit on their capacity set by ventilation requirements, it would be impossible to admit even a few extra persons without increasing the likelihood of death for all occupants.

In conclusion, therefore, it can be stated that an individual can clearly improve the possible protection available to himself and his family. He cannot, however, no matter how much money he spends, guarantee his survival.

There is very little indeed that an individual can do to improve the protection afforded by his home against the effects of blast. Although careful adherence to government advice will provide some protection against fallout, whether or not it will provide sufficient protection is more a function of the distance from the explosion and its associated fallout than any added precautions that can be taken.

The construction of shelters specifically designed to protect against fallout and/or blast will in most cases provide increased protection. This increased protection is minimal, if indeed it even exists, for Types 1a, 1b and 2 of the designs suggested by the government.[1] Type 3 offers marginally increased protection against blast and fallout and Type 4 is comparable to other commercial shelters, which offer, at a high price, the chance, but no guarantee, of survival in the short term. No shelter can guarantee survival beyond this.

The extent to which commercial shelters afford basic protection against blast and fallout is very much a function of where they are in relation to the point of explosion, as is the case for the protection offered by a person's home. In all cases, however, there is a better chance of survival for those in the shelter as compared to those in their own homes. In areas nearest to the point of explosion where the blast and fire damage is severe, i.e. up to 2.5 miles from a 1 MT air burst, the survival of those in the shelter is by no means guaranteed, due to the various problems outlined earlier of ventilation, blast-proof entry hatches, fire-storms, etc. There is no way of accurately assessing the likelihood of survival but it will certainly be greater than that of those people who are relying on their own homes for protection – since these will almost certainly all be killed by the blast, heat or fallout within a matter of days.

In areas of only moderate, light or no blast and fire damage, the shelter is likely to provide increased protection against blast and fire and will act as an effective fallout shelter, providing a much higher level of protection than refuge rooms under the stairs. The problems of effective warning and psychological stress cannot be minimised, however.

The consumer has no guidance as to what level of protection to provide for his family and his expenditure of a minimum of £10,000 in providing such a shelter can be based on no guaranteed information, nor can he be certain that the shelter would function according to the manufacturer's claim when he actually needed it to.

Finally, it must be pointed out again that even the most elaborate and effective protection provided by the shelter will only have enabled its occupants to survive the short-term effects of a nuclear explosion. The medium- and long-term effects are no less daunting and the survivors will emerge out of their shelter to find a world lacking in the basic essentials for life and civilisation. These medium- and long-term effects and the possibilities for regeneration are discussed in detail in the following chapter.

References

1. Home Office, *Domestic Nuclear Shelters: Technical Guidance* (HMSO, London 1981).
2. Home Office, *Domestic Nuclear Shelters: Advice on Domestic Shelters Providing Protection Against Nuclear Explosions* (HMSO, London, 1981).
3. S. Glasstone and P.J. Dolan (eds.), *The Effects of Nuclear Weapons* (United States Department of Defense and United States Department of Energy: 3rd edition, Castle House, Tunbridge Wells, 1980).
4. Home Office, *Protect and Survive* (HMSO, London, 1980).
5. I. Tyrell, *The Survival Option: A Guide to Living Through Nuclear War* (Jonathan Cape, London, 1982).
6. C. Sibley, *Surviving Doomsday* (Shaw & Sons, London, 1977).
7. LATB Study Group, *London After the Bomb* (Oxford University Press, Oxford, 1982).
8. E. Alley, 'Short-term Measures' in *Nuclear Attack: Civil Defence*, eds. RUSI (Brassey's, Oxford, 1982).
9. L. Godfrey, 'The Sceptical Buyers Guide to Fall-out Shelters' in *Observer* Magazine, 4 July 1982, pp. 24-7.
10. Office of Technology Assessment, *The Effects of Nuclear War* (Croom Helm, London, 1980).
11. P. Goodwin, *Nuclear War: the Facts on our Survival* (Ash & Grant, London, 1981).
12. Stockholm International Peace Research Institute, *Nuclear Radiation in Warfare* (Taylor & Francis, London, 1981).

5 RECOVERY AND RECONSTRUCTION

The short-term effects of a nuclear war have been discussed in detail in Chapters 2, 3 and 4. The death and destruction in the first few weeks following the explosion, however, are but the short-term consequences of nuclear attack. Equally immense problems will face the survivors in the medium and long term and there can be no guarantee of survival even after the first few weeks have passed. Very little has been written concerning recovery and reconstruction; however, the horror of the short term should not blind us to the fact that many millions of people will survive the immediate short-term problems and they will be in need of certain basic essentials in order to carry on living.

This chapter is concerned therefore to identify the possibilities for reconstruction of an economy and society in the UK subsequent to a nuclear attack and in particular to consider the possibilities and problems involved in the reconstruction of people's homes and the resumption of the domestic infrastructure that is considered essential in our society today — i.e. the provision of a clean water supply and a constant supply of energy.

A brief summary will also be given of the other major problems likely to be facing survivors in the medium and long term. Needless to say, these problems will also be faced by those who had the added protection of a specially designed shelter to help them withstand the short-term effects of the explosion. The problems of food, water supply and social readjustment will be equally difficult for everyone, whatever their circumstances had been in the days immediately after the attack. People's basic needs after the first 14 days of self-help would be for water and food. Those whose homes have been destroyed will be in need of shelter, although it is likely that many of those who were within the zones of total and heavy destruction at the time of the explosion would have died in their homes. The most likely persons to have survived, albeit with varying doses of lethal radiation, will be those in areas of moderate and light damage as well as the more remote areas where there was no blastwave or fire damage at all. In these areas people's homes will still be standing, although they will possibly have windows and doors blown in, tiles blown off the roof and cracks in the masonry.

Estimates have been made by a variety of sources[1,2,3] as to the likely number of casualties and survivors – these vary obviously according to the scale of the attack experienced as well as more minor factors such as time of the attack, types of weapon used, etc.

Duncan Campbell[1] notes that at a NATO civil defence committee conference in May 1977, UK Home Office staff gave a detailed assessment of likely casualties in the UK after a 180 MT, 80 targets attack. Immediate deaths would be 3 million to 4 million and serious injuries would be 5 million to 9 million (all assumed to die quickly). A year later only two-thirds of the population would have survived, the remaining millions having died from radiation, exposure, starvation and disease.

Openshaw and Steadman[2] calculated casualties for the 'Square Leg' scenario assuming different protective factors across the country. Casualties caused by blast alone amounted to 23.6 million. Fallout casualties ranged from 0.4 million to 17 million depending on the average protective factor. Burns injuries were not calculated. Total number of deaths therefore ranged from 24 million to 40.6 million.

This chapter is primarily concerned with the possibilities for the reconstruction of people's homes. The provision of food and water are, however, the primary essentials; without these people would have no further needs for shelter at all. A brief description is therefore provided of the problems and possibilities for food and water supply.

Recovery – Who Will be Responsible?

The first aspect to be considered when talking in terms of recovery from a nuclear war, are the factors that led to the war in the first place. There are a variety of different political possibilities subsequent to a nuclear war. If the aggressor has succeeded in forcing his will on the UK – either after a single explosion or after an all-out attack – it will be his responsibility to run the country and manage its long-term future. As is the case with any military takeover of a country, the enemy would impose his own government on the country and determine its course of action. If the USA and its allies had emerged as 'victors' – if there can indeed be any such thing subsequent to a nuclear war – then they would need to cope with the problems of the defeated enemy as well as their own. A much more likely outcome is that of the mutual destruction of both combatants – neither side having the capacity to bring the other to a point of submission. In this case the countries would be responsible for repairing their respective structures as best they could. Other nations of the world, particularly those possessing key resources, would then emerge as the dominant nations.

Given the assumption that the UK has not been occupied by a foreign power, to what extent will there be an effective government capable of providing suitable relief for survivors and to what extent must an individual rely upon his own resources? As Finkelstein[4] notes, the shock and devastation produced by a nuclear catastrophe, with its total disruption of normal life and activities, and with the problems of mere animal existence uppermost in everyone's minds, would tend to make the individual household a unit striving to survive in isolation from, and in competition with, the rest of society. It is unlikely that large amorphous centres of population would develop spontaneous co-operative ventures although pre-existing closely-knit communities may well do so.

If effective government is to reassert itself it must be seen to be in control immediately after the attack. The extent to which this is possible depends partly upon the civil defence plans and preparations made prior to any attack and partly upon the destruction caused by the attack — if the majority of central and dispersed government head-quarters as well as the communications systems have been destroyed, then there is very little chance of any form of government being rapidly established.

The preparations made by the government for its survival after a nuclear attack were outlined in Chapter 3. Dispersed governmental responsibilities lie with the Sub-regional Commissioners, County Controllers and District Controllers (peacetime Chief Executives) who, in theory, should be safe within their protective accommodation, along with those staff and representatives who have been allotted a designated wartime task and thus a degree of protection. Several assumptions have to be made however, if this theoretical control is actually to materialise subsequent to a nuclear attack; first, that the protective accommodation is available for the personnel and does in fact provide the necessary protection. It was found in the 1980 Square Leg exercise, for example, that 3 of the 17 SRHQs had no proper headquarters at all. The second assumption is that the correct personnel are in the shelter at the time of the attack — if it is a surprise attack or an unauthorised release of a nuclear weapon, it is extremely unlikely that all necessary personnel would be anywhere near the shelter; if an attack came outside of normal working hours, most of the necessary personnel would be at home, in all probability some distance away. It is extremely unlikely that more than a matter of a few hundred yards could be travelled in the time available before the fallout commenced and questionable whether a person would leave his family to their fate in order to try to reach his local headquarters, not even knowing for instance whether it still existed. Even if there had been a period of increasing hostility between the superpowers it is unlikely that key staff would be on constant standby night and day to cope with a possible nuclear attack.

Although the government has issued a series of instructions to county and district authorities, in many cases these authorities, already hard-pressed in terms of staffing and finance, have paid only token lip service to their civil defence responsibilities. An example of this is the survey that authorities are expected to have carried out on the protective qualities of residential accommodation in their areas. As explained in Chapter 3, only 2 of the 43 authorities approached had even started the survey and many stated quite simply that they had no intention of carrying it out at all, due to lack of staff and money.

With regard to training of personnel there is at present only one remaining college, that at Easingwold, which provides expert tuition in civil defence matters. During 1983 only 700 persons, including local authority scientific advisers, members of the Red Cross and St John's Ambulance Brigade, WRVS and others were expected to attend courses at the college.[5] Staffing is limited: as an example, there is not even a full-time or qualified librarian[6] to cope with the ever-increasing volume of literature that is currently available on civil defence.

Training of civilians as volunteers has been emphasised by the current Conservative government as being an important aspect of civil defence, but no information is publicly available as to the number of volunteers who have been recruited.[7] It must be expected, however, in the event of a surprise attack, that the fully trained person, or civil defence volunteer, is as likely to be killed or injured as any other person and it would be incorrect to assume that all those who have been trained to assist with the recovery will be there to do so.

Assuming that at least some semblance of decentralised government has survived the nuclear attack, it will be essential that a reliable system of communication is established in order for regional and national organisation to re-emerge. It will also be essential rapidly to establish some form of communication to the civilian population – to give instructions and to encourage popular commitment to the restoration of the government and the economy.

The Emergency Communication Network within areas comprises a network of buried teleprinter and telephone cables and a smaller number of radios. Whether or not such equipment would survive the initial EMP effects is not known; certainly any equipment switched on would be destroyed. The fact that the network is largely buried underground does increase the chance of its survival. However, communications over longer distances, whilst essential for the location and distribution of goods, are much more likely to be destroyed, by EMP as well as blast effects. Laurie[8] states that microwave cones only need to be damaged or moved out of the correct alignment to fail. Since the microwave network is largely overground, the effects of blast would be very significant. Military and other essential communications are being hardened wherever possible against the effects of the EMP.

In view of all these uncertainties regarding the establishment of local, regional and national government, it would seem likely that individuals would have to rely very much on their own resources and capabilities in the first few weeks after the attack. If this situation continued for any length of time, the social cohesion and behaviour essential for the re-establishment of a caring society would break down irreparably.

The Provision of Food and Water

The primary concern of an individual after a nuclear attack will be the provision of food and water for himself and his family. He knows quite simply that without these items he will die. A certain amount of food will have been stored in his home although it is likely to have been consumed within the first 14 days after the attack. Other nearby sources of supply would include neighbouring homes which were empty, local shops, allotments and vegetable gardens.

Supplies of water would be extremely limited in the absence of a mains water supply; small amounts could be obtained from hot and cold water tanks, toilet cisterns, garden water butts, but this would provide only a very short-term supply indeed. The resumption of a piped supply of water (as will be seen later) will be impossible in the short term and the government anticipates using water tankers *inter alia* to help distribute the necessary supplies[9] – to 'organise ... the replenishment of domestic water, perhaps using standpipes, tanks, tankers, local wells, streams and other sources'. Given that failure will have occurred at many pumping stations due to the electricity supply being cut off, the use of standpipes would be very limited indeed. As the BMA point out, however,[10] even in peacetime tankers available in the UK could carry and distribute water for essential purposes to just

2 per cent of the population. Given the added problems of lack of fuel and debris-blocked roads, this method would provide only minimal assistance for the civilian population.

Gamma radiation does not affect the purity of water, although supplies can be contaminated by the fallout. Once the fallout has settled to the bottom, however, the water above it should be safe for consumption: even so, shallow pools and ponds would be likely to have fallout particles in suspension near the surface and would be dangerous to use. Underground sources of water are unlikely to be contaminated and a series of boreholes would be expected to provide the major source of water in the UK after a nuclear attack. As mentioned above, the major problem will be to ensure distribution of water to those people who need it.

The provision of food is also essential if human life is to continue. Experiments have shown[11] that 500 calories a day will prevent starvation but make work impossible, 1,000 calories a day will keep a person physically healthy but the minimum required for sustained work is 1,500 calories. Compared to the current average daily consumption in the UK of 2,500-3,000 calories, there is clearly room to reduce the daily calorie intake without causing any harm, and in all probability increasing the healthiness of many overweight individuals.

At present in the UK we import 55 per cent of our total food requirements. This situation is sustainable in the present sophisticated economy which incorporates a great deal of world trade. After a nuclear attack, the UK would have to become self-sufficient in its food supplies. Assuming a change in diet to incorporate a much higher percentage of cereal and vegetables and a drastic reduction in the supply of meat protein it should be possible to grow enough food to maintain a healthy population. Laurie[8] makes the following calculations – that we have 18,300,000 arable acres in the UK. If each produces 4,000 plant calories a day (current rate is 8,000 plant calories per day) and there are 40,000,000 survivors then only 14,700,000 acres are needed to supply the population with plant calories. At the minimum meat ration of just over half an ounce per day, enough meat protein could be produced on the remaining 3,600,000 acres to feed 72,000,000 which is almost twice the minimum requirements. The BMA, however,[10] are not so optimistic about the prospects for agriculture, noting that changes in ozone concentrations and the atmospheric effects of forest fires, gas and oil wells would severely reduce crop yields, concluding that 'it appears unlikely that agricultural crop yields would be sufficient to feed more than a small part of the remaining population so many of the survivors of the initial effects of nuclear war could die of starvation in the immediate first post-war years'.

Deep-sea fish would be unlikely to be affected by fallout and Laurie[8] estimates that even half of the current catch would be sufficient to provide minimum protein for 64,000,000 people.

The major problem is clearly not the production of food but rather its distribution to where it is needed. It is likely that since it will be the rural areas where most of the survivors are, the problems would not be as severe as if it was the current population distribution that required feeding. The most severe feeding problems would be immediately after the attack, before fresh supplies could be grown; government supplies are held in buffer depots around the country. Irradiated animals are fit to eat provided they are slaughtered before they fall sick and animals grazing on contaminated pasture in the month after the attack would be fit to eat provided the carcasses were properly bled and offal and bone discarded. Standing crops in the early stages of growth are damaged by radiation but otherwise are safe to eat if washed clean of dust. Drinking fresh milk after an attack could cause high doses of radiation especially in children. Processed dairy products, such as hard cheeses, have a much reduced radioactive mineral content.

Present methods of farming, reliant as they are on the petroleum and chemical industries, would have to be substantially changed. Harvesting and drying grain are heavily dependent on power supplies and it is unlikely that there would be sufficient tools or skilled personnel to resort to the more traditional methods of reaping. Farming would have to become much more labour intensive. Simple methods of repair and replacement of mechanical parts will be needed if any of today's labour-saving equipment is to continue in use. Substitutes for the current, chemical-based fertilisers would need to be found. Crop rotation would have to be increasingly practised to prevent the development of diseases currently controlled by pesticides and herbicides.

The government sets out its plans in ES1/79[12] for post-attack feeding of the population. These include food control in the period before nuclear attack (assuming there is sufficient warning time) and stockpiling of 'cereals, soya and other animal feed; oils and fats, and sugar as sources of post nuclear attack food supply'. Flour, sugar, fat, yeast and special biscuits are permanently stockpiled by the MAFF. Feeding equipment is held in depots and would be released to county councils in the pre-attack period (assuming there is sufficient advance notice of the attack). Central government and the regional and sub-regional headquarters would be responsible for the supply of food and the controllers of counties and districts for its distribution, conservation and control.

Detailed arrangements are set out for the various bureaucratic functions involved with the distribution of food. There is, however, very little discussion of where the food is actually going to come from both in the immediate and longer terms, although it is stated that 'the supply of food would include the procurement and distribution of new imports'. This would seem a particularly optimistic view, given that most of our European food suppliers are likely to be caught up in the same nuclear attack and that long-distance shipping from the USA and Canada is extremely unlikely to continue.

Once the basic needs of food and water have been met, a major concern will be the provision of adequate shelter for the population, particularly as the autumn and winter seasons would increase the need for basic protection against the elements.

The Provision of Shelter

As stated earlier, the major tasks in the initial provision of shelter will be of repairing, patching and making do, using materials from destroyed or semi-demolished buildings. The construction of new buildings would only be commenced at a much later date. Not only would houses need to be mended but communal buildings, roads, railways, etc. would all need to be restored to use. There would therefore be much opportunity for the use of manual, largely unskilled, labour; building skills, together with those relating to agriculture, would be amongst the most highly valued in the post-attack recovery period.

The Supply of Building Materials

The first source of supply of building materials would be those cannibalised from existing buildings. Bricks, timber and roof tiles, as well as many fittings, would be easily available; it is unlikely however that significant amounts of glass would be found in semi-destroyed buildings since it is so vulnerable to the effects of the blastwave. Fresh cement or other bonding agents would also be needed.

The need for new buildings would soon emerge as a matter of priority – not only people's homes but also new power stations, water pumping stations and treatment works, hospitals, schools, sewers, etc. A source of new supplies would be needed to carry out a reconstruction programme on any large scale. The provision of such materials will not necessarily be an easy matter. Consideration is given below to four main materials commonly used in house construction in the UK – bricks, timber, cement and glass.

Building bricks are made predominantly of clay and are fired at high temperatures. They are a bulky and heavy product to transport and their production is therefore fairly broadly distributed throughout the UK, with the densest concentration of brickworks in the Midlands. Virtually all the bricks used are produced in this country, the cost of transport preventing any effective scale of imports. The number of brickworks in the UK has been declining, however; in 1938 there were 1,147 brickworks in Great Britain (producing 6,939m bricks), by 1969 this had fallen to 544 (producing 6,734m bricks) and by 1973 it was down to 357 (producing 7,183m bricks, i.e. more than the original 1,447 brickworks).[13] There are over 150 companies involved in brick-making, although the London Brick Company is by far the most important, supplying 40.9 per cent of the market and with a complete monopoly on fletton bricks which are made from Lower Oxford Clay and are extremely important to the building industry. Since the number of producers is fairly large and fairly well distributed throughout the country, the problem of supply of bricks for reconstruction after a nuclear war would not be insurmountable. Although modern factories use electrically fired kilns and the bricks are made by an automated process, hand-making of bricks is not an unknown skill; hand-made bricks are still produced for certain high-value sectors of the market. Traditional firing techniques could be used to replace more modern methods until a mains power supply had been restored. Production levels would be very low compared to current levels.

The production of timber for use in construction, however, would be more problematic in the UK, since such large quantities are imported – only 5 per cent of the softwood used in the UK is home produced, 26 per cent of the hardwood, 2 per cent of the plywood and block-board and 28 per cent of the particle board.[14] The main suppliers of timber to the UK are Finland (15.44 per cent of UK timber imports); Sweden (13.72 per cent); Canada (12.27 per cent); USSR (9.2 per cent); Portugal (3.99 per cent); and Malaysia (3.2 per cent). Of these countries, Finland and Sweden are likely to be suffering the conse-quences of fallout after any European-based nuclear war. Canada is far more likely to divert all its spare resources to the USA, with whom it has a land boundary, and the USSR, given that all military scenarios envisage this country to be the UK's most likely combatant, is scarcely likely to continue exporting timber to the UK, especially when she would in all probability be concerned with her own reconstruction. Other suppliers lie many thousands of miles away, and the UK could hardly rely on the efficient functioning of a commodity market to purchase imports.

The indigenous supply of timber is likely to have suffered in the event of a large-scale nuclear attack, particularly if it took place at a time when the forests were susceptible to fire. Timber, like bricks, is also heavy, bulky and difficult to transport. Local supplies, however limited, would have to be relied on to provide any essential timber needed in reconstruction. Relatively unskilled labour would be required to produce timber suitable for construction purposes; cutting and planing would have to be done by hand until the restoration of electricity permits more modern methods to be used once more.

The constituents of cement, i.e. lime, alumina, silicon and iron oxide, are widely found throughout the UK, although there is a noticeable concentration of supplies in the south east. There are only 32 establishments producing cement in the UK and it is not easily transported.

It may be possible or necessary for more elementary forerunners of cement to be used once again. Some form of bonding agent would certainly be needed even for basic mending of houses since there is no possibility of re-use of existing materials. The vast majority of cement used in the UK is home produced and cement production could clearly be developed locally if supplies of the raw materials were available. Transportation would again prove a problem in those areas where local supplies of the raw materials were not available, since the raw materials are bulky and heavy to transport.

The most common form of damage to houses following a nuclear attack would be broken windows. As Table 2.1 showed, all windows will be broken by the blastwave up to 13 miles from a 1 MT air-burst explosion. Since glass could not be purloined from other semi-destroyed houses it would be necessary in the short term to replace glass windows and doors with other materials which are to hand – planks, boarding, plastic sheeting would be amongst the more obvious alternatives.

There are at present 688 glassworks throughout the UK, 603 of which are small (employing less than 100 people); almost 80 per cent of total production is accounted for by the largest 33 plants – each of which employ over 400 workers.[15] Glass is made of sand mixed with an alkaline flux, usually soda or potash, and requires heating to high temperatures. The raw materials are cheap and widely available throughout the UK – the production process, however, is highly auto-mated today, although there are still a substantial number of smaller works throughout the country where old skills and equipment may possibly be found. Until mains power supplies were restored, older methods of production would have to be relied upon.

In summary, therefore, it would seem that production of bricks, glass and cement could possibly be continued on a small, decentralised scale throughout large areas of the country, relying on unskilled labour to produce on a labour-intensive basis that which had previously been produced on an automated, capital-intensive basis. A far smaller output would be achieved, however, compared to current production levels, but this would be only of minor importance in meeting the needs of war-damaged Britain. There would, however, be no other source of materials: demand would have to be adjusted accordingly. The opera-tion of such production processes would inevitably come under the direction of the government, since the development of a market economy such as we have today would take many years if not decades to re-establish. The availability of timber would remain a problem until a means of importing foreign supplies had been re-established or newly-planted trees had matured in the United Kingdom – both of which are fairly long-term prospects. In the short term, all available trees, regard-less of their aesthetic value or tree preservation orders, are likely to be felled to provide urgently needed timber.

Only when or if a reliable source of power supplies became available could production be commenced at anything approaching current levels of production. It is a vicious circle, however, in that power supplies cannot be recommenced until the power stations have been rebuilt and this large-scale reconstruction requires large inputs of power to produce the raw materials to carry out the construction.

Methods of Construction

Current methods of construction are based upon the use of power tools and petrol-driven machinery as well as the use of skilled manual labour. Certainly the production of large-scale multi-storey buildings of rein-forced concrete requires a large input by heavy machinery. The con-struction or restoration of small brick-built houses, however, would rely much more upon the skills of bricklayers, carpenters, plasterers, electricians, etc., using predominantly handtools. These handtools are still likely to be in plentiful supply after a nuclear attack. Tools such as cement mixers and power drills could be replaced with manual labour. In the absence of power supplies, any new construction in the period after the bomb is likely to be on a small scale requiring neither large-scale excavation or multi-storied construction. Space will no longer be at a premium since vast acreages in the centre of cities will have been reduced to rubble and in addition there will be far fewer people to house.

Priorities for new construction would be restoration of roads and railways, water pumping stations and treatment works, power stations and the electricity supply network. Considerable engineering expertise is likely to be necessary in the construction of this infrastructure and construction will inevitably be on a more limited scale given the paucity of resources available.

The Restoration of Essential Services

If there is to be any semblance to today's life-style in the recovery period after a nuclear war, it is not enough simply to repair the shells of people's homes, patch up the furniture and dig the gardens. A supply of clean water, a continual power service and a fuel supply have become regarded as essentials for modern living and as much a part of a house as the doors or walls, and would in all probability continue to be so regarded in the aftermath of a nuclear war. What then are the possibilities of restoring these services to individual households? Obviously the possibilities for restoration will be better in some areas than others – i.e. those furthest from the bomb damage will have no blast or heat damage to the actual infrastructure providing the service, although the centralised source of provision, i.e. pumping station or power station, may be out of action; in areas nearer to the explosion, the water mains and power lines may also have been destroyed.

Restoration of Water Supply

There is very little doubt that the mains water supply will be one of the first casualties of a nuclear war – the government states as much in their circular *Water Services in War*.[9] 'It can be said with absolute assurance that any widespread nuclear attack would quickly disrupt the distribution system for domestic and industrial water.'

There are various causes of failure of the system and these include:

– blast and fire damage to water mains within people's homes.
– blast damage to the underground water mains – i.e. ground shock in

areas close to the crater of a ground-burst weapon. The fracture of a sizeable main would lead to severe water loss and flooding.
— failure of electrical power supplies will prevent the pumping of water and the purification of water.
— blast damage to buildings containing control equipment for local and national supply networks.
— lack of regular maintenance (viz. 1982 water strike).
— blast damage to reservoirs themselves (not very likely since many are situated in remote areas, however the *London After the Bomb* study[3] noted that in the government Square Leg exercise the reservoirs within the West London chain together with their associated treatment works were within the area of heavy damage. The North London installations in the Lea Valley were within the zone of repairable damage but were unlikely to be repaired in the foreseeable future).

The extent to which piped supplies could be restored is partly a function of the nature of the damage that has been suffered. Wells and boreholes as well as distribution by tanker would have to be relied upon until a reliable piped supply was again in operation. This could easily take months or years in some areas, especially if it is failure of the power supply that is the major cause of disruption. Fractures to pipes and even damaged reservoirs can be mended fairly promptly given sufficient expert guidance, labour and basic raw materials; the provision of a mains power supply could take much longer, especially in areas where power stations need to be rebuilt. Even if individual generators were used in each pumping station, these would need to be first obtained and secondly, fuelled, in some way. Even when a piped supply was eventually re-established it is doubtful whether water would be available for 24 hours per day as at present: a rationing system would in all probability be used to keep down consumption levels and associated costs.

Restoration of Fuel Supplies

The most commonly used fuels (as opposed to power) used in the UK today in the domestic sector are mains gas, electricity, oil and coal. Minor sources of fuel include bottled gas and wood. The regular supply of all four main sources will be non-existent after a nuclear war. The sources of disruption will again be various and include damage involving both the source of supply and its distribution to people's homes.
The coal industry is the least likely of the energy industries to be

affected by a nuclear war, with its underground installations largely undamaged. Although modern pits rely heavily upon mains electricity to power machinery, the old methods of manual extraction are still well known, even if no longer used, and could be used again. Production levels would obviously not be as high and the demand for coal is likely to have increased, if this is the first form of fuel to become available. A major problem would be distribution of the coal from the relatively few pitheads to where it is needed. Large quantities are currently moved by train; it is likely however that damage to railway track, engines and rolling stock would be heavy, particularly in urban areas, and that large amounts of fuel would be required to power the BR engines currently in use. Movement of coal would thus present substantial problems.

The effects of a nuclear attack upon the oil industry would have repercussions throughout the entire economy of the UK since it is a basic fuel source used *inter alia* in power stations, for road, rail and air transport, as the basis for the petrochemical industry and also for much domestic heating. Key installations for oil production and refining would be prime targets in any counterforce attack as well as an all-out attack on the UK. These installations could not be restored except by the use of modern technology (unlike coal mining, for example). Restoration of supplies, however, would be a major priority for any post-war government. Domestic consumption would have little priority as compared to the needs of transportation and power generation; supplies to individual homes would be virtually unknown for many years.

Gas is widely used as a means of cooking and heating in homes throughout the UK today. Supplies of gas, however, are likely to be cut off after a nuclear war due to damage to the distribution network and/or the production installations. Virtually all of the UK gas supply now comes from the North Sea and the wells here and their feeders would be vulnerable to attack. The gas comes ashore at only four points in the UK (St Fergus, Easington, Theddlethorpe and Bacton). Precautions have been taken in view of the vulnerability of this situation and an independent underground power supply has been installed at Bacton to keep it working through periods of emergency. If the supply line is damaged before the gas comes ashore there is very little that can be done to restore the supply and as with oil supply only high technology can be used to restore it. This would in all probability take a matter of years and again the domestic consumer is unlikely to be afforded high priority when there are so many pressing national industrial needs.

Electricity has a dual role as both a fuel-providing energy for heating and cooking in the home – as do oil, gas and coal – and also as a unique source of power for lighting and all manner of domestic as well as industrial equipment. Virtually all homes in the UK have an electricity supply and in many homes it is the only source of energy. Since its predominant role is that of a power supply it is dealt with separately below.

Restoration of Power Supplies

Electricity is the common source of power used in both the domestic and industrial situation. It is produced in the UK in 222 power stations (variously fired by coal, oil, nuclear and hydroelectric power) and transmitted via the national grid throughout the country. It is possible to produce electricity independently of the national grid, using small generators, banks of batteries, windmills, etc., but the vast majority of all electrical power consumed in the UK today is produced centrally in the large power stations. The small generators commonly used to supply power where none other is available are themselves powered by diesel oil and these would therefore not be a viable option in the time of oil famine after a nuclear attack.

It is unlikely that all 222 power stations will be destroyed, since many of them lie at some distance from centres of population or counterforce targets. The 20 nuclear power stations and the 25 largest conventional power stations (each producing between 1 and 2 GW per annum) are themselves likely to be targets of any attack aimed at crippling recovery of the country.

Even those that are undamaged, however, could not continue to operate once their stocks of fuel – coal or oil – had run out. Only the hydroelectrical power stations in Scotland could be safely assumed to be able to continue functioning. At present these supply less than 2 per cent of the UK electricity supply. It would be months or years, if ever, before sufficient oil was available to commence production at today's oil-fired stations. The coal-fired stations, often with rail links to local pitheads, would represent the most realistic possibility for resumption of a centralised supply.

Far greater and more extensive damage is likely to be done to the distribution network, which is likely to be damaged by the electromagnetic pulse as well as blast and fire. The exact effects of the electromagnetic pulse have not been fully investigated, as the 1963 partial test ban treaty was imposed before its effects had been fully documented. It is generally assumed however, and the government states as much in its Emergency Services Circular on *Energy Supplies in War*,[16] that the EMP would render the entire national grid inoperative by the induction of excessive currents in the network of transmission lines. Suitable arresters need to be installed prior to any attack if power lines are to be protected from EMP. Damage by blast alone, however, is sufficient to cripple large areas of the country's network. Pylons and overhead transmission lines would be susceptible to the high-speed winds associated with the blastwave and many switching stations and substations would be damaged beyond repair in the same way as other buildings. There is however spare capacity built into the system and it may be possible, in those areas which have two or three potential means of supply, that one set of supply links will be undamaged.

The overall effect of even a limited attack, however, would be a drastic reduction in the power available for consumption in the UK. As I. Tyrell states,[17] however, much less power will be needed. Millions of homes will have been destroyed, entire cities may have largely vanished, shops and factories would stand empty and silent — the dead have no needs.

Given that only limited power supplies are available, connection of domestic users to the mains supply is likely to be afforded only very low priority. Restoration of supplies to industry, hospitals, water supply, transportation, schools, etc., is likely to have priority over the connection of the individual household.

In conclusion, therefore, the provision of shelter after a nuclear attack is likely to be a very makeshift, piecemeal effort, dependent largely upon an individual's initiative and DIY abilities. Vast inequalities will exist between those whose homes in the more remote areas are virtually unscathed and those who have become homeless refugees.

Patching up and mending houses that are still standing using cannibalised materials is likely to be the major form of restoration of people's homes in the post-attack period. Construction of new homes will be severely limited due to lack of priority status and lack of building materials. Building materials are likely to be scarce and production would be very limited until power supplies could be fully restored. Priority for whatever materials are available would not be given to new houses for the homeless. Sources of timber would be very limited indeed in the absence of world trade.

Even in those homes where there has been relatively little or no structural damage, the services contained within those homes are likely to be seriously curtailed or non-existent — water, gas and electricity supplies would not exist for many months, if not years. Houses would be largely unheated and lit only by candles and other primitive forms of lighting. Dampness and draughts would prevail in the wintertime.

Building skills would be of prime importance in the time after a nuclear attack. Methods of construction would revert to the small-scale techniques currently employed in the construction of one- or two-storey family homes. Multi-storey development and industrialised building systems will not be possible in the absence of power and fuel to operate the large machinery necessary for such construction. The current government emphasis on individual house rehabilitation will have provided an experienced workforce on a small-scale decentralised basis which is ideal in time of recovery from a nuclear attack.

The problems encountered in the provision of shelter must be set in the context of the likely conditions prevailing in post-attack UK. Radiation sickness and other bacterial infections will have caused widespread death and disability among the population. Irreparable damage will have been done to the environment with possible destruction of the protective ozone layer of the atmosphere, widespread destruction of forests and contamination for centuries of the land around destroyed nuclear power stations. Industry and the economy will have been completely destroyed and the present way of life will have become a thing of the past.

Genetic mutation could continue for generations. Lack of food and water will cause starvation and death for many millions, especially the young and old. Starving, disease-ridden people are not rational; in all probability many will have watched loved ones, often children, die an agonising death. One of the government's most difficult tasks (of which it is fully aware) will be to protect itself against the survivors.

References

1. D. Campbell, *War Plan U.K.* (Burnett Books, London, 1982).
2. S. Openshaw and P. Steadman, *Predicting the Consequences of a Nuclear Attack on Britain: Models, Results and Public Policy and Implications* (Environment and Planning C, Government and Policy 1, 1983), pp. 205-8.
3. LATB Study Group, *London After the Bomb* (Oxford University Press, Oxford, 1982).
4. L. Finkelstein, 'Long-term Measures' in RUSI (eds.), *Nuclear Attack: Civil Defence* (Brassey's, Oxford, 1982).
5. Written Answer to Parliamentary Question: Hansard, 31 March 1983, p. 267.
6. Written Answer to Parliamentary Question: Hansard, 14 July 1983, p. 398.
7. Written Answer to Parliamentary Question: Hansard, 30 March 1983.
8. P. Laurie, *Beneath the City Streets* (Granada Publishing, London, 1970; revised and updated, 1983).

9. Home Office, *Water Services in War*, Emergency Services Circular ES6/1976 (HMSO, London, 1976).
10. British Medical Association's Board of Science and Education, *The Medical Effects of Nuclear War* (John Wiley & Sons, Chichester, 1983).
11. R.S. Pogrund, *Nutrition in the Post-attack Environment* (Rand Corporation, Santa Monica, 1966).
12. Home Office, *Food and Agriculture Controls in War*, Emergency Services Circular ES1/79 (HMSO, London, 1979).
13. Monopolies and Mergers Commission, *Building Bricks – A Report on the Supply of Building Bricks* (HMSO, London, 1976).
14. Timber Trade Federation, *Yearbook of Timber Statistics 1979* (Timber Trade Federation, London, 1979).
15. Business Statistics Office, *Business Monitor 1979* (HMSO, London, 1979).
16. Home Office, *Energy Supplies in War*, Emergency Services Circular 5/76 (HMSO, London, 1976).
17. I. Tyrell, *The Survival Option: A Guide to Living Through Nuclear War* (Jonathan Cape, London, 1982).

6　CONCLUSION

The aims in writing this book were fourfold. First, to analyse in detail the physical damage caused to residential housing by the use of nuclear weapons. Secondly, to ascertain the extent to which residential housing would provide suitable protection against the effects of nuclear weapons. Thirdly, to consider the effectiveness of the current civil defence measures to provide protective accommodation in the event of nuclear war; and fourthly, to suggest possible ways, if indeed there are any, of improving the available protection for the civilian population in time of nuclear war. The first three aims have already been covered in detail and their conclusions will be summarised briefly below.

The intention in producing this book is to make available objective findings and to answer the basic question – 'If I stay at home in accordance with government advice, what protection will my house provide in the event of nuclear war?' The book is written entirely without political motivation or bias and as far as possible the controversy surrounding the holding and use of nuclear weapons has been avoided. Likewise, the arguments as to whether the provision of civil defence increases or decreases the likelihood of nuclear war have also been avoided. This book however has been concerned to ascertain whether or not the current civil defence plans will prove at all effective in the event of a nuclear attack upon the UK.

The main conclusions are:

1. In the event of a large-scale nuclear attack upon the United Kingdom, the vast majority of houses will be destroyed or rendered uninhabitable by the effects of blast and fire.
2. The existing housing stock can provide only very limited protection against the effects of the blast and heatwaves. In the extensive areas of total destruction and heavy damage it will offer no protection at all.
3. There is no appreciable way in which the present housing stock can be improved so as to provide effective protection against blast and fire.
4. People's homes will afford some protection against radioactive fallout, although not to the extent claimed by the government. If government advice is followed regarding construction of an inner

refuge room and provision of adequate supplies, the chances of survival (in the short term) will be increased.

5. Government figures regarding the effects of a nuclear attack on the UK underestimate the death and damage likely to be incurred.

6. There are severe limitations on the likely effectiveness of commercial nuclear shelters, particularly against the effects of blast and fire. They do afford greatly increased protection, however, against radioactive fallout. Their true effectiveness can only be finally ascertained in the event of a nuclear attack.

7. The possibilities for widescale regeneration of the economy and industry following a nuclear attack are extremely limited. The rebuilding of people's homes would be one of the few sectors of the economy, however, where some form of recovery would at least be feasible.

8. There can be no comparison at all between the conventional warfare experienced in the Second World War and nuclear warfare.

If there is to be any understanding of the effects of nuclear war it must first of all be realised that there is no comparison between this and the conventional bombing experienced by civilians in the UK in the Second World War. Two of the main effects of nuclear weapons – the intense heatwave and radioactive fallout – were simply not produced by the conventional high explosive bombs dropped on UK cities. Nor does the blastwave compare to the force of that associated with nuclear weapons. In the absence of extensive fires and lethal fallout, digging out of survivors from their homes, offices or factories was a relatively easy task. Radioactive contamination of food and water supplies did not exist. Widespread radiation sickness and death did not exist. There were very few burns casualties to be dealt with by hospitals. Medical services continued to function throughout the war – the British Medical Association[1] states quite categorically in its report, *The Medical Effects of Nuclear War* 'The NHS could not deal with the casualties that might be expected following the detonation of a single one megaton weapon over the U.K. It follows that multiple nuclear explosions over several, possibly many, cities would force a breakdown in medical services across the country as a whole.'

The first area of investigation was into the type and extent of physical damage likely to be suffered by typical houses in the UK after the explosion of a nuclear weapon. The two main effects of nuclear weapons which affect the physical structure of buildings are the heatwave and blastwave; radiation only affects living cells and is therefore a source of danger to human beings themselves rather than their homes. The effects that these two phenomena will have are set out in summary in Table 2.1 (page 12) for different size weapons. More detailed figures are provided in Tables 2.2, 2.3, 2.4, 2.5, 2.6 and 2.7. For an average-sized bomb, however (1 megaton is commonly regarded as the average size, even though it is 80 times larger than that dropped on Hiroshima), houses will be completely destroyed up to 2.5 miles from the point of explosion and severely damaged for a further 2.5 miles. One of the recent government exercises assumed that a total of 200 MT explosive was dropped on 80 targets – this would mean that even for a total of 80 MT (i.e. 1 MT per target) the area over which houses would be destroyed completely would be 6,280 square miles – and this would cover some of the most densely populated areas of the UK. Many of the occupants of the houses in this area, even if following government instructions to hide in a strengthened inner room, would be killed outright or trapped in their homes, only to die later of a lethal radiation dose. Even beyond these areas of total and severe damage, there are further areas extending a total of 15 miles from the point of explosion (i.e. covering an area of 706 square miles) of moderate and light damage. Houses here would have doors and windows blown in, roof tiles stripped off and cracks in masonry, the severity of the damage varying according to the nature of construction and proximity to the explosion.

The extent of the area damaged by fire goes beyond that covered by the blastwave's most serious effects. Houses up to eight miles from the explosion of a 1 MT bomb would experience temperatures sufficient to cause spontaneous ignition of paper and fabrics and thus capable of starting fires in people's homes. The development of mass fires remains a distinct possibility, although it is lightly dismissed by the Home Office. Given the current fashion for extensive glazing in people's homes and the high combustibility of modern furniture, the development of mass fires would seem a distinct possibility, especially given the relatively large size of today's weapons. Any buildings within the area covered by mass fires would be razed to the ground and all persons in the area burned or asphyxiated.

Estimates of blast and burn casualties have been made by various sources, including the generally accepted definitive American sources[2,3] and the UK government. The figures produced by the Home Office, however, are consistently lower than those produced by other sources. In the case of blast casualties this is due to the fact that the Home Office assumes, first, that smaller areas are affected by the blastwave of a given size weapon and secondly, that the given overpressure levels kill fewer people. In the case of burns casualties, the Home Office casualty model omits any consideration of burns – caused both directly and indirectly (two-thirds of the fatalities on the first day at Hiroshima were due to burns). Using the American basis for calculations, deaths caused by blast damage alone in the Square Leg attack amounted to 23,600,000[4] – over 40 per cent of the population.

It is often argued that a counterforce attack, i.e. an attack upon military and other strategic targets only, would cause relatively little destruction of residential areas. It can be seen from Figure 1.1 (page 6), however, that in these densely populated islands military targets and major centres of population lie only a matter of a few miles from each other, unlike the USA and USSR where military targets are many hundreds of miles from centres of population. Since relatively large weapons would be used against hardened military targets, residential areas are unlikely to avoid being severely damaged.

The second area of investigation was to ascertain the extent to which residential housing would provide suitable protection against the effects of nuclear weapons. The weapons effects against which protection is needed are the heatwave, blastwave and radiation.

There are three major causes of injury by the heatwave: first, the intense flash of light causing temporary blindness; second, the direct effects of burns caused by the heatwave on exposed human beings; and third, the indirect effects of injury caused by fires. If people are in the protected refuge room of their homes they will be afforded complete protection against the first two of these effects, since they will neither be looking directly at the source of the explosion, nor will the heatwave be able to reach them. Only if a person is standing in front of a window or open door in line with the source of explosion will he be in any danger of receiving direct burns. The vital aspect in securing this protection is being given (and heeding) sufficient warning to seek the safety of one's home or another suitable building. There is no guarantee however that a person's home will provide protection against the effects of fires, since it is perfectly possible that it will catch fire itself – either by being in close proximity to other burning buildings, or by being caught up in a mass fire or simply by the heatwave shining through windows and causing spontaneous ignition of the house's contents.

There has been very little guidance from the government as to exactly what protection people's homes offer against the blastwave; virtually all advice given concerns protection against radiation. The fact is that people's homes offer very little protection against blast. Most houses in the UK would be flattened or irreparably damaged with an overpressure of 4 p.s.i. – this would be experienced at up to 5 miles from the explosion of a 1 MT bomb and 11 miles from a 10 MT bomb. There is virtually nothing an individual can do to strengthen the resistance of his house against such pressure levels. If the occupants of a house are hiding in a strengthened refuge room they will not necessarily be killed by the collapse of their home on top of them, although it is very doubtful whether they would survive the subsequent fire and fallout hazards. It is extremely unlikely that anyone will ever come to dig them out. In those areas where overpressures are not so great it will be safer to be indoors rather than outdoors since the high winds can blow people into heavy objects or vice versa causing direct physical injury and possibly death. Protection will need to be sought by those indoors from the dangers of flying glass. The only 'safe' option for a householder whose home is likely to suffer severe blast damage is to be as far away from it as possible in an area where the blastwave has declined in its destructive power. This, however, is a far cry from government advice to remain in your own home.

The third effect of a nuclear explosion against which protection is needed is radiation. This is the most commonly discussed effect and the one against which government advice is primarily directed. The protection afforded by a building against radiation can be expressed as the 'protective factor' (PF) of that building. This is the factor by which the dose rate received by a person in the building is reduced as compared to that received by a person standing outside. The Home Office has produced a series of protective values for different types of dwelling – ranging from 10 for a bungalow to 45 for a terraced two-storey house. These values are calculated on the basis of a complicated formula involving size, type and density of wall, roof and floor construction. Several assumptions have been made in producing these figures, however, which bring their validity into doubt, including the assumptions that no fallout enters the building or is deposited on walls, window sills or other projections; that windows and doorways have been blocked; that a strengthened refuge room has been built in the best place in the building; and that its occupants follow government instructions implicitly. These assumptions will clearly lead to the true PF of the building being considerably less than that estimated by the Home Office. American sources and studies carried out in the UK which allow for blast damage in the PF calculations produce a more realistic average figure for the PF of 5 or 6 for most people's homes (in rooms other than the basement). As shown in Table 3.5 (page 70), even this is sufficient to reduce the dosage of radiation to a non-lethal level in the short term (the development of cancers in the longer term cannot be ruled out, however) for those persons in areas of moderate, light or no blast damage.

If sufficient supplies of food and water are provided and government instructions are closely followed, then the protection afforded by people's homes in areas of moderate and light blast damage will be sufficient to prevent immediate death and will reduce the accumulated doses to relatively low amounts. For many survivors, however, the PF of their home is a largely academic matter since their houses have been totally destroyed or so severely damaged as to afford no protection whatsoever. Exposure in the open air with radiation levels initially as low as 400 rads/hour for even two hours would ensure sufficient absorption to be assured of a prompt and painful death.

The third area of investigation was to consider the effectiveness of current civil defence measures in providing protective accommodation in the event of a nuclear war. In 1968 the government finally abandoned the notion that civil defence should be able to provide effective relief for the survivors, realising that this was no longer possible. Instead it concentrated on providing the means for the survival of an effective system of government to ensure recovery after the attack. Evacuation policies for the mass of the population have been rejected since there is nowhere upon the surface of the UK mainland that could be guaranteed to be immune from the effects of nuclear attacks. The government's advice to stay at home in improvised protective accommodation is the only other option available, assuming that the government is not willing to spend large sums of money on providing blast-proof shelter places for the population, as has been done by some of the other European nations. Even assuming that such protective shelters had been provided for the population, sufficient warning cannot be guaranteed to ensure that people have time to reach them.

As has been shown above, however, people's homes provide virtually no protection against blast and fire and only limited protection against radiation. It must be concluded therefore that current government plans for civilian protection in the event of nuclear war have very little value indeed and it would seem to be virtually chance whether or not an individual survives.

One option available to an individual who would rather not leave the question of his ultimate survival to chance is to purchase, at considerable expense, a blast-proof underground shelter designed to provide full protection against the effects of nuclear weapons. Claims by the manufacturers for the protection afforded by these shelters cannot be factually substantiated and it is noted that claims for similar structures often showed surprisingly large discrepancies – all such claims should therefore be treated with an element of caution. All shelters have potential problems and weaknesses inherent in their design which may limit their effectiveness – these include water seepage, blockage of ventilation systems, blockage of exit routes, provision of fully blast-proof hatches and protection against external fires. In addition there are the problems of sufficient warning and psychological stress which undermine any shelter scheme. These commercial shelters would all provide virtually complete protection against radiation unless prolonged attack caused supplies of food and water to run out. No matter how much money an individual spends he cannot guarantee his survival. It should be noted, however, that even those who survive in the short term will emerge to find a world lacking in the basic essentials for life; continued survival through the medium and long term can be by no means assured.

Government plans for its own protection, albeit in a somewhat reduced capacity, have formed a major item of civil defence expenditure since 1968. Blast-proof fully equipped underground shelters both in London and at decentralised locations have been provided – whether officials would have time to get to them is questionable in the event of a surprise attack. The capacity of the vital warning network and communications systems to withstand the effects of the electromagnetic pulse must be seriously in doubt. Without effective communications the establishment of any regional or national level of government after a nuclear attack would be virtually impossible.

The government have made token plans for survivor relief – covering *inter alia* the provision of food and water, fuel and power, health facilities and for dealing with aspects of environmental health and homelessness. These plans are outlined in the Home Office Emergency Services circulars and are in many cases seemingly oblivious to the likely nature and scale of the problems involved. With regard to food, for example, little consideration is given to the problem of where food supplies will come from once existing buffer stocks have run out. With regard to water supply the assumption that tankers and standpipes could meet the needs of a population seriously affected by radiation sickness and enteric diseases is clearly wrong. The BMA's complete rejection of government's plans for the provision of medical facilities comes only after a thorough and extensive study of the practicalities involved.

Not only are the plans lacking in content, they are also largely ignored by those county and district councils who are meant to be carrying them out. Lack of staff and finance, as well as political commitment in some cases, have meant that in many cases only token lip-service is paid to their civil defence duties. One of the recent civil defence exercises had to be cancelled due to the fact that many local authorities refused to join in. Nuclear-free zones are still in operation in 144 local authority areas.

Survival in the medium and long terms cannot be automatically assumed once the initial post-attack period is over. Many people would even question the very desirability of surviving the short term given the future that they are likely to be facing. What if anything can be done, therefore, to improve the protection available to the civilian population in the event of nuclear war?

As noted above there is very little that an individual can do to increase his own protection unless he is willing to spend in the order of £10,000 to provide private blast-proof and fallout facilities. Even then there is no guarantee that sufficient protection will be provided. There is also very little that he can do to his existing home to improve the extremely limited protection it offers against blast and fire; by following government instructions, however, he can increase the protection that it affords against radiation and may be able to reduce the radiation received to tolerable levels. In areas of high initial radiation, however, few homes, even with strengthened refuge rooms, would provide sufficient protection against radiation. Again it would seem that survival in the short term is very much a matter of chance – whether a weapon is exploded near your home (i.e. within 15 miles), whether you are at home at the time, whether the house has windows directly facing the source of explosion, whether any warning was given or heard, what the prevailing windspeed and direction were, whether it was raining or foggy at the moment of detonation, etc.

Whether or not the government can do anything to improve the current level of protection available to the individual in the event of nuclear war is a highly contentious issue. The government would argue that a high level of defence spending on nuclear and conventional weapons and remaining within the NATO alliance are the most effective forms of protection against nuclear war. The European peace movements would say that only by totally abandoning the use of nuclear weapons can the dangers of nuclear war be avoided.

Leaving aside these more general considerations, there are also arguments as to whether a more effective form of civil defence could be found than that currently in force, in particular, whether a policy of evacuation or the provision of deep shelters would be a more effective form of protection. Both schemes have their drawbacks – evacuation to a 'safe' place is commonly argued to be impossible given the limited size of the UK. Since blast and fire rather than fallout are the cause of most deaths, many millions of persons living close to likely targets would most certainly be safer moved to areas where only fallout (if anything) is likely to be experienced. Such evacuation would require detailed planning and would take several days to achieve. Whether or not evacuation of the civilian population would act as a spur to an aggressor is again highly questionable. The provision of fully equipped and stocked deep shelters in urban areas to provide protection against blast, fire and fallout has been rejected as a possibility on the grounds of cost. Given the likely warning time that will be available to the general public, it is also doubtful whether they would actually save many lives. If the population were sent into the shelters in a period of high tension, this may again be interpreted as evidence of an intention to launch a pre-emptive strike and spur an aggressor to strike first.

Assuming that the stay-at-home option is the only feasible one, can anything else be done to improve the protection available for civilians? The improvement of the warning system would seem to be the most effective improvement since this gives people a chance to seek protection against the blast and heatwaves. Hardening of the system to withstand the electromagnetic pulse would be essential. Requirements to provide protected places in all new buildings constructed and encouragement to employers to provide protection for their workforce are measures frequently employed by our European neighbours. Moves towards the encouragement of volunteer training have already been made by the present government. Plans made for the relief of survivors after an attack would need to be extensively revised as they are largely inadequate in their current form. This all entails high levels of expenditure which at present appear to be politically unacceptable.

Even if the government were to spend large sums of money on providing protection for the civilian population before, during and after a direct nuclear attack upon the UK, it would be to little avail, for there can be no effective defence against such an attack. As long as the UK holds her own and NATO nuclear weapons she is likely to be subject to a direct attack rather than just experience the fallout from attacks on other countries. The loss of millions of lives and the destruction of industry and the economy, as well as the disturbance of global ozone and other environmental balances, would ensure that civilisation and the way of life as known today would never be regained. Nuclear war must never become a credible option and it must be understood that nothing, least of all our homes, would provide any protection against it.

References

1. British Medical Association's Board of Science and Education, *The Medical Effects of Nuclear War* (John Wiley & Sons, Chichester, 1983).
2. Office of Technology Assessment, Congress of the United States, *The Effects of Nuclear War* (Croom Helm, London, 1980).
3. S. Glasstone and P.J. Dolan (eds.), *The Effects of Nuclear Weapons* (United States Department of Defense and United States Department of Energy; 3rd edition, Castle House, Tunbridge Wells, 1980).
4. S. Openshaw and P. Steadman, *Predicting the Consequences of a Nuclear Attack on Britain: Models, Results and Public Policy and Implications* (Environment and Planning C, Government and Policy, 1983), pp. 205-8.

APPENDIX 1: THE NATURE OF NUCLEAR REACTIONS

In order to understand more fully the destructive power of nuclear weapons it is necessary to understand a little of the physical processes involved. Outlined below are the basic physical facts concerning the explosion of nuclear weapons.

Matter comprises an assembly of atoms of various *elements* interspersed in space at relatively great distances from one another. An *atom* of an element is the smallest particle which can show the individual chemical properties of that element. An atom is extremely small and most of the matter contained in each atom is concentrated in a central *nucleus*. A nucleus always carries one or more positive electrical charges (*protons*) and is normally surrounded by a number of negatively charged particles (*electrons*). Because of the repulsive forces between positive charges protons cannot approach each other closely and in a nucleus containing more than one proton *neutrons* (particles with no electrical charge) are required to prevent the protons flying apart. The larger the nucleus, the greater is the excess of neutrons over protons needed to hold the nucleus together.

All atoms of one element contain the same number of protons but may have different numbers of neutrons. Thus there may be several atomic species of the same element and these are known as *isotopes*. Those isotopes which contain too many or too few neutrons are unstable or radioactive and disintegrate by expelling neutrons or electrons in order to restore the balance needed for stability. The results of this disintegration are:

(i) expulsion of alpha particles (nucleus of the element helium without its two outer electrons)
(ii) expulsion of beta particles (i.e. electrons expelled at high speed from the nucleus)
(iii) gamma rays (an electromagnetic radiation like X-rays but of much shorter wavelength)

The isotope U235 of uranium and PU239 of plutonium are unstable (i.e. radioactive) and their atoms disintegrate by expelling alpha or beta particles with gamma rays from the nuclei.

The energy released in an atomic reactor or in the detonation of a

127

nuclear weapon is caused by neutron absorption of the uranium or plutonium atom, destabilising that atom, which then disintegrates with the further emission of neutrons which maintains the chain reaction.

The three main features of the fission process are:

(i) the large amount of energy released at each fission
(ii) the radioactivity of the isotope resulting from splitting of the original isotope
(iii) the release of several neutrons (this makes the process practically feasible since these neutrons can be used to start a chain reaction).

In order for the *fusion process* to take place, extremely high temperatures have to be generated and the only known way at present of producing the required temperatures is that achieved by the explosion of an atomic (A) bomb. Thus every H-bomb has two stages: first, a fission bomb, which acts as a trigger, secondly, a fusion mixture, which is ignited by the heat caused by the trigger.

A temperature of several million degrees centigrade is reached in the detonation of a nuclear fission weapon. In these circumstances the nuclei of the rarer hydrogen isotopes (deuterium and tritium) have enough energy of motion to overcome the repulsive forces and are able to fuse together i.e. *nuclear fusion*. On an equal weight-for-weight basis, the fusion energy is about 2½ times as large as the energy of fission of U235. Helium gas is the main product of a thermonuclear detonation and is *not* radioactive (known therefore as the 'clean' bomb), but very high-speed neutrons are emitted which collide with other atoms. When they collide with nitrogen atoms in the atmosphere they release a very intense and penetrating form of gamma radiation (flash) and although, if it is a ground burst, there will be intense radioactivity in some of the ground material, this decays rapidly in a few days.

The *neutron bomb* is a small hydrogen bomb in which the components are arranged so as to augment greatly the nuclear radiation. Only small quantities (a few grams) of deuterium and tritium are needed. By exploding the bomb at 500m above ground the blastwave is not strong enough to destroy strongly constructed buildings. However, 80-90 per cent of the whole of the energy of the hydrogen bomb comes off in the form of neutrons, which are highly destructive of human tissue.

There will be some radioactive fallout from the small atomic device needed to provide the trigger for the fusion but since this is relatively small, the amount of fallout will be correspondingly decreased. The intense neutron radiations coming at the instant of the explosion are short lived, and after a few weeks they will have almost all decayed into harmless end products.

APPENDIX 2: CIVIL DEFENCE IN OTHER COUNTRIES

It is only in the twentieth century that the nature of warfare has entailed the need to protect civilian populations. In earlier times the bulk of death and destruction was suffered by military personnel and equipment. Civil defence programmes have therefore been instigated in over 100 countries. Although the civil defence preparations of Switzerland and Sweden are perhaps the best known, many other European countries, as well as the USA and USSR, have made extensive civil defence preparations. These preparations are described in detail in a variety of sources (Business Statistics Office, British Medical Association's Board of Science and Education, and Calder) and a brief summary of the preparations undertaken in other European countries are set out in Table A.1.

It can be clearly seen from Table A.1 that the majority of European countries, with the exceptions of France, Italy and the UK, are undertaking thorough if not extensive programmes of civil defence. Virtually all countries have increased their spending over the last three to four years. In Sweden and Switzerland civil defence has been a long-established national priority forming an intrinsic part of the defence policy of those countries. Shelters are built to an exceptionally high standard and are available for a large proportion of the population. In Switzerland, in addition to the extensive shelter provision, there are 88 underground hospitals complete with operating centres and a total of 74,000 protected hospital beds. One of the largest of the Swiss projects is the Sonnenberg Tunnel on the outskirts of Lucerne. Here there are bunks and complete facilities for over 20,000 people including a hospital, foodstores and generators. Warning and monitoring organisations are efficient and extensive and the entire population receives civil defence training.

Sweden is likewise well advanced in its civil defence organisation. It considers civil defence to be part of a total defence concept incorporating military defence, economic defence and psychological defence in addition to civil defence. Information is extensively disseminated through the media and all Swedish men and women between the ages of 16 and 65 are obliged to serve in civil defence. In addition there are 170 civil defence voluntary organisations.

Current policy is to provide individual shelters and large public shelters. Public shelter places are now available in the larger towns for a total of 100,000 people and there are individual shelters available for 5,000,000 people (total population 8,300,000). All industrial firms employing more than 100 people must have civil defence arrangements. Concern has also been expressed about chemical warfare and to date 2,000,000 gas masks have been issued with a further 300,000 per annum under production.

Clearly the emphasis throughout those European countries who are making civil defence preparations is upon the provision of shelters to protect the civilian population *in situ* rather than evacuating large sections of the urban population. Indeed, the policy in Sweden has been changed from the early plans for evacuation to the present *in situ* shelter programme. Likewise in Denmark, where the government relies on its shelter programme to ensure public survival, although evacuation plans have been made.

The NATO policy with regard to European civil defence is the stay-put policy followed by the UK government, although most governments have given some consideration to a policy of evacuation and made limited plans. A major policy document, for example, was produced by the West German government in 1972 suggested that very vulnerable areas should be evacuated. Likewise the UK government is said to be reconsidering the possibilities for a policy of evacuation in the UK. Clearly in those relatively small countries where there is a high population density, evacuation presents a far less attractive policy for effective civil defence than in those countries where there are extensive tracts of sparsely populated countryside. This is notably the case for the USA and the USSR, where evacuation policy forms the basis for civil defence.

Donnelly[1] notes that Soviet civil defence policy is to retain in the urban areas only those persons essential to the running of key industries and for basic rescue and repair. Blast-resistant, well-equipped shelters are provided for key workers at their place of work as well as for all leadership and command personnel. It is estimated at present that at least 50 per cent of the essential working population have suitable shelter places with other temporary places being available. Construction of shelters continues in order to fulfil the stated requirement. The key to survival for the bulk of the population, however, is clearly mass evacuation. Soviet authorities claim to be able, given adequate warning time and prior practice, to evacuate large cities in two to five days. Exactly how the millions of evacuees are then maintained in the rural areas is not well documented. Training in elementary civil defence is

Table A.1: European Civil Defence Preparations

Country	Population (millions)	No. of Shelter Places Public	No. of Shelter Places Private	No. of Shelter Places Provided by Firms
United Kingdom	55	None	Minimal	None
W. Germany	62	2,000,000	Not known — although householders are encouraged to provide their own protection	None
France	54	None	ditto	None
Norway	4	170,000	1,600,000	200,000
Holland	14	6,500,000		All firms employing more than 30 persons obliged to provide shelter places
Denmark	5	2,500,000 compulsory in new buildings & in residences with more than 2 families		None
Sweden	8.3	Provision for over 5m of the population with a further 250,000 shelter places being built per annum		All firms employing more than 100 persons
Switzerland	6.5	6,300,000		All industries have civil defence organisations
Italy	57	None	Minimal	None

N.A. = Not Available.

Table A.1: Contd

| Annual Expenditure | | Warning: | | Monitoring |
Actual (£m)	% Milit: Budget	No. of Sirens	Testing	No. of Monitoring Posts
£27m shortly to be incrsd. to 45m (49p per head of population) (php)	0.002	18,000	Rarely	872
£147m £2.33 php	1-2	82,000	Twice per year	N.A.
Minimal		All towns with over 4,000 pop.	Monthly	4,000
£22m £5.50 php	4	Adequate number	Annually	N.A.
£37m £2.62 php	N.A.	All settlements with over 1,000 pop.	Monthly	1,400
N.A.	4+	700+	N.A.	400
N.A.	N.A.	All towns with over 5,000 population	N.A.	N.A.
£61m £9.38 php	7+	N.A.	N.A.	
£54m 0.94 php (for fire and civil protection)	2.5	Public warning only in Rome and Venice	N.A.	1,625

Table A.1: Contd

	Training		
Full-time Civil Defence Workers		Number of Volunteers	Evacuation
Minimal		Minimal	No plans
N.A. although it is estimated that 600,000 would be needed in the Federal Civil Defence Services in the event of war.			Plans for most vulnerable areas
Civil Protection Defence Corps comprised of military reservists (number unknown)		50,000 + thousands of employees who undergo civil protection training	Very vulnerable areas would be evacuated
All citizens are liable for Civil Defence Service. Peacetime strength is 113,000			N.A.
Civil Defence Corps has peacetime strength of 180,000		Over 100,000 industrial workers have received training in civil defence tasks	N.A.
23,000 Conscripts		90,000	Plans have been prepared
All citizens obliged to serve in civil defence. Peacetime strength is 250,000. A further 65,000 in the industrial civil defence organisations			Early plans for evacuation have now been replaced by a shelter policy
All citizens obliged to serve in either civil or military defence — mandatory strength is 420,000			N.A.
Training only of government employees having civil protection duties			None

given to everyone and serious attempts at training procedures are carried out with military/civilian civil defence exercises. All organisations are required to practise any emergency procedures they would have to undertake in time of war. In addition there are volunteers (estimates vary from 5 million to 15 million) who carry out civil defence duties. Extensive warning and monitoring procedures have been established. The civil defence programme currently accounts for 1 per cent of the overall defence budget plus additional payments from the other sectors of government involved, e.g. the Ministry of Education is responsible for certain training expenditure.

The election of President Reagan in 1980 brought added stimulus to the somewhat confused subject of civil defence in the USA. A \$4.2 billion programme for crisis relocation (i.e. evacuation) was approved in March 1982. In the 1950s, prior to missile delivery of weapons, there was a city evacuation system in the USA based on adequate warning time given by the slow journey of the bomb-carrying aircraft. No plans were made for fallout protection. In the 1960s, due to the development of weapon delivery by missile (the ICBMs and the SLBMs), evacuation was replaced with a policy emphasising fallout shelters. The number of spaces provided eventually exceeded the number of Americans, although the demand and supply of such shelter places was far from matched. Eventually the need for blast protection was realised and shelter stocks were disposed of. The 1980s, as emphasised by the crisis relocation programme, have seen government policy swing once again in favour of mass evacuation. Blast sheltering is provided only for leadership and command personnel (being too expensive to provide for the general population). Public acceptance of the need for civil defence in the USA is proving hard to achieve. Instruction in civil defence subjects has ceased to be taught in state schools and no national volunteer organisation exists for civil defence purposes.

Reference

1. C. Donnelly, 'Preparing to Survive – the Soviet Union'; in Royal United Services Institute (ed.), *Nuclear Attack: Civil Defence* (Brassey's, Oxford, 1982).

APPENDIX 3: GOVERNMENT CIRCULARS ON CIVIL DEFENCE

Home Office Civil Defence Circulars (CDC)

5/69   Earmarking of Church Premises
2/70   Requisitioning of motor vehicles in a war emergency; arrangements for supplies of motor fuel for essential services in war
4/71   Essential Service Routes

Home Office Emergency Services Circulars (ES)

1/72   Home Defence 1972-76
2/72   Police Deployment in a War Emergency
3/72   Police Deployment in a War Emergency
4/72   Police Home Defence Training
5/72   Local Authority Scientific Staff
7/72   National Arrangements for dealing with Incidents involving Radioactivity (The NAIR Scheme)
8/72   Regional and Local Authority Scientific Staff
1/73   Home Defence Regional and Sub-regional Boundaries in England and Wales
2/73   Counter Sabotage Planning
3/73   Home Defence Planning Assumptions
4/73   Amendments to Financial Arrangements
5/73   Local Authority Scientific Staff
6/73   Home Defence College, York
7/73   Machinery of Government in War
8/73   Government Wartime Communications for Local Authorities Financial Arrangements
9/73   Essential Service Routes
1/74   Civil Defence Act, 1948 – Subordinate Legislation
2/74   Home Defence College, York
3/74   Biological Weapons Act, 1974
4/74   Food and Agriculture Control in War
5/74   War Emergency Planning for the Fire Service
6/74   Protection of Key Points

7/74	Key Point Protection
8/74	Local Authority Scientific Staff: Home Defence College – Incidental Expenses
9/74	Regional Co-ordination of Local Authority Home Defence Planning
10/74	Public Survival under Fallout Conditions
11/74	Armed Forces in War
12/74	Home Defence Training for the Police
1/75	Nuclear Weapons
2/75	Information Services in War
3/75	Police Manual of Home Defence
4/75	Construction Work and Building Materials in War
5/75	Communications in War
6/75	Post Office Telephone Preference Scheme
1/76	Fallout Protection in War
2/76	Community Organisation in War
3/76	Briefing Material for Wartime Controllers
4/76	Ports and Shipping in War
5/76	Energy Supplies in War
6/76	Water Supplies in War
7/76	Homelessness in War
8/76	Environmental Health in War
9/76	Advice to the Public on Protection against Nuclear Attack
1/77	Organisation of the Health Service for War
2/77	Inland Transport in War
3/77	National Arrangements for Incidents Involving Radioactivity (The NAIR Scheme)
4/77	Home Defence College, York
5/77	Public Survival under Fallout Conditions
6/77	Home Defence Planning Guidance – 1977 Onwards
1/78	Transmission of Radiological Information in Wartime
2/78	Earmarking of Buildings for War Planning
3/78	Home Defence College, York
1/79	Food and Agriculture Controls in War
2/79	Wartime Communications for Local Authorities
3/79	Emergency Communications Procedures
4/79	Home Defence Training for the Police
5/79	Satellite Accidents
1/80	Local Home Defence Training
2/80	Advice to the Public – Protect and Survive
1/81	Civil Defence Review

2/81   Community Organisation in War; Voluntary Effort in Civil Defence

3/81   Protection of the General Public in War; Survey of the Protective Qualities of Residential Accommodation

1/82   Financial assistance toward the Home Defence Activities of the Red Cross and St John at County Level

2/82   Basic Training of Local Authority Scientific Advisers

BIBLIOGRAPHY

Alley, E., 'Short-term Measures' in *Nuclear Attack: Civil Defence*, ed. RUSI (Brassey's, Oxford, 1982)

British Medical Association's Board of Science and Education, *The Medical Effects of Nuclear War* (John Wiley & Sons, Chichester, 1983)

Britten, S., *The Invisible Event* (Menard Press, London, 1983)

Building Research Establishment, *Fires in Dwellings – an Investigation of Actual Fires. Part I – Hazards due to Ceiling and Roof Construction*, BRE Current Paper CP51/77 (Department of the Environment, London, 1977)

Building Research Establishment, *Fires in Dwellings – an Investigation of Actual Fires. Part II – Hazards from Ground-floor Fires. Part III – Physiological Effects of Fire*, BRE Current Paper CP80/78 (Department of the Environment, London, 1978)

Burhop, E., *The Neutron Bomb* (CND, London, 1981)

Burton, J., *Dear Survivors* (Frances Pinter, London, 1982)

Business Statistics Office, *Business Monitor 1979* (HMSO, London, 1979)

Calder, N., *Nuclear Nightmares* (Penguin, London, 1979)

Campbell, D., *War Plan U.K.* (Burnett Books, London, 1982)

Clarke, M., *The Nuclear Destruction of Britain* (Croom Helm, London, 1982)

Clayton, J.K.S., *Training Manual for Scientific Advisers*, Scottish Home and Health Department (HMSO, Edinburgh, 1978)

Committee for the Compilation of Materials on Damage caused by the Atomic Bombings in Hiroshima and Nagasaki, *Hiroshima and Nagasaki: The Physical, Medical & Social Effects of the Atomic Bombings*, trans. E. Ishikawa and D.L. Swain (Hutchinson, London, 1981)

Crossley, G., *British Civil Defence and Nuclear War: A critical Assessment with Reference to Economic Consequences*, Peace Research Reports No. 1 (Bradford University School of Peace Studies, 1983)

Draft Statutory Instrument, *The Civil Defence (Grant) (Scotland) Amendment Regulations 1983*

Draft Statutory Instrument, *Draft Civil Defence (General Local Authority Functions) Regulations 1983* (HMSO, London, 1983)

Draft Statutory Instrument, *Draft Civil Defence (Grant) (Amendment) Regulations 1983* (HMSO, London, 1983)

Draft Statutory Instrument, *The Civil Defence (General Local Authority Functions) (Scotland) Regulations 1983* (HMSO, London, 1983)

Finkelstein, L., 'Long-term Measures' in RUSI (ed.), *Nuclear Attack: Civil Defence* (Brassey's, Oxford, 1982)

Galtung, J., *Environment, Development and Military Activity* (Global Book Resources, London, 1982)

Gaskell, R., *Nuclear Weapons: the Way Ahead* (Menard Press, London, 1981)

Glasstone, S. and Dolan, P.J. (eds.), *The Effects of Nuclear Weapons* (United States Department of Defense and United States Department of Energy: 3rd edition, Castle House, Tunbridge Wells, 1980)

Godfrey, L., 'Seminar for Survival', *Protect and Survive Monthly* (May 1981)

Godfrey, L., 'The Sceptical Buyers Guide to Fall-out Shelters', *Observer* Magazine, 4 July 1982, pp. 24-7

Goodwin, P., *Nuclear War: the Facts on our Survival* (Ash & Grant, London,

1981)

Greater London Council, *Greater London Housing Condition Survey 1981* (London, 1981)

Hansard, *House of Commons Debate 24 March 1983*, pp. 1088-1103

Hansard, Written Answer to Parliamentary Question: Hansard, 31 March 1983, p. 267

Hansard, Written Answer to Parliamentary Question: Hansard, 14 July 1983, p. 398

Hansard, Written Answer to Parliamentary Question: Hansard, 30 March 1983, p. 145

Harries, R. (ed.), *What Hope in an Armed World?* (Pickering and Inglis, Basingstoke, 1982)

Hodgson, R. and Banks, R., *Britain's Home Defence Gamble* (Conservative Political Centre, London)

Home Office, *Home Defence Planning Assumptions*, Emergency Services Circular ES3/73 (HMSO, London, 1973)

Home Office, *Machinery of Government in War*, Emergency Services Circular ES7/73 (HMSO, London, 1973)

Home Office and Scottish Home and Health Department, *Nuclear Weapons* (HMSO, London, 1974)

Home Office, *Energy Supplies in War*, Emergency Services Circular 5/76 (HMSO, London, 1976)

Home Office, *Water Services in War*, Emergency Services Circular ES6/76 (HMSO, London, 1976)

Home Office, *Environmental Health in War*, Emergency Services Circular ES8/76 (HMSO, London, 1976)

Home Office, *Food and Agriculture Controls in War*, Emergency Services Circular ES1/79 (HMSO, London, 1979)

Home Office, *Protect and Survive* (HMSO, London, 1980)

Home Office Scientific Advisory Branch, *Protective Qualities of Buildings* (HMSO, London, 1981)

Home Office, *Domestic Nuclear Shelters* (HMSO, London, 1981): advice on domestic shelters providing protection against nuclear explosions.

Home Office, *Protection of the General Public in War*, Emergency Services Circular ES3/81 (HMSO, London, 1981)

Home Office, *Domestic Nuclear Shelters: Technical Guidance* (HMSO, London, 1981)

Home Office, *Civil Defence Review*, Emergency Services Circular ES1/81 (HMSO, London, 1981)

Jackson, A., *Feeding the United Kingdom after a Nuclear Attack – a Preliminary Review* (Journal of the Institute of Civil Defence, October 1980)

de Kadk, E.J., *British Defence Policy and Nuclear War* (Frank Cass, London, 1964)

Katz, A.M., *Life after Nuclear War: The Economic and Social Impacts of Nuclear Attacks on the United States* (Ballinger, Cambridge, Mass., 1982)

Laurie, P., *Beneath the City Streets* (Granada Publishing, London, 1970; revised and updated, 1983)

LATB Study Group, *London After the Bomb* (Oxford University Press, Oxford, 1982)

McMahan, J., *British Nuclear Weapons, For and Against* (Junction Books, London, 1981)

Medical Campaign against Nuclear Weapons and Medical Association for the Prevention of War, *The Medical Consequences of Nuclear Weapons* (Cambridge, 1981)

Ministry of Defence, *Statement on the Defence Estimates 1982 Parts I and II* (HMSO, London, 1982)

Monopolies and Mergers Commission, *Building Bricks — A Report on the Supply of Building Bricks* (HMSO, London, 1976)

New Statesman, *Britain and the Bomb* (New Statesman, London, 1981)

Office of Technology Assessment, Congress of the United States, *The Effects of Nuclear War* (Croom Helm, London, 1980)

Openshaw, S. and Steadman, P., *Predicting the Consequences of a Nuclear Attack on Britain: Models, Results and Public Policy and Implications* (Environment and Planning C, Government and Policy 1, 1983)

Peterson, J. (ed.), *AMBIO, A Journal of the Human Environment*, Royal Swedish Academy of Sciences/Pergamon Press, vol. XI, nos 2-3 (1982)

Pogrund, R.S., *Nutrition in the Post-Attack Environment* (Rand Corporation, Santa Monica, 1966)

Radical Statistics Nuclear Disarmament Group, *The Nuclear Numbers Game* (Radical Statistics, London, 1982)

Rogers, P., *As Lambs to the Slaughter* (Arrow Books, London, 1981)

Royal United Services Institute (ed.), *Nuclear Attack: Civil Defence* (Brassey's, Oxford, 1982)

Sibley, C., *Surviving Doomsday* (Shaw & Sons, London, 1977)

Simpson, T., *No Bunkers Here* (CND, London, 1982)

Stockholm International Peace Research Institute, *Yearbook 1980, World Armaments and Disarmament* (Taylor & Francis, London, 1980)

Stockholm International Peace Research Institute, *Nuclear Radiation in Warfare* (Taylor & Francis, London, 1981)

Stockholm International Peace Research Institute, *Yearbook 1982: World Armaments and Disarmaments* (Taylor & Francis, London, 1982)

Thompson, E.P., *Beyond the Cold War* (Merlin Press, London, 1982)

Timber Trade Federation, *Yearbook of Timber Statistics 1979* (Timber Trade Federation, London, 1979)

The Times, 21.6.1983, p. 1

Tucker, A. and Gleisner, J., *Crucible of Despair — the Effects of Nuclear War* (Menard Press, London, 1982)

Tyrell, I., *The Survival Option: A Guide to Living Through Nuclear War* (Jonathan Cape, London, 1982)

Zuckerman, S., *Nuclear Illusion and Reality* (Collins, London, 1982)

INDEX